Philip Odei Tettey

The truth of Biter Device and child custody Struggle

Philip Odei Tettey

The truth of Biter Device and child custody Struggle

The Truth of Biter Devoice

Blessed Hope Publishing

Imprint

Cover image: www.ingimage.com

Publisher:
Blessed Hope Publishing
is a trademark of
International Book Market Service Ltd., member of OmniScriptum Publishing Group
17 Meldrum Street, Beau Bassin 71504, Mauritius
Printed at: see last page
ISBN: 978-613-7-93607-8

The Biter truth of Biter Devoice and child custody struggling

Parental alienation is a problem that most often arises when parents engage in bitter and extended child custody struggling. At times intense feelings of anger and mistrust are common when parents are struggling to transition from marriage wave of emotions surrounding divorce into a co-parenting relationship. Most often some parents experience less anger and anxiety over such times rather they make efforts to co-parent in a way that it will be healthier and more productive for the children.

The Parental alienation occurs when a child is influenced by other parent often called the *alienator* as to completely reject the other parent often known as the *target one*. In most severe cases, alienation results in the other child completely rejection of the target parent. Usually, the reasons for the rejection are unfounded or unjustified, according to parental educator and author

Owning to the intensity of emotions that will erupt during the lengthy process of separation and divorce, so many parents will experience strain and frustration within the parent's relationship to the said child. This will allow some parents engage in harmful and destructive behaviours that eventually lead to the natural consequence of the child rejecting the said parent from other parent. For better explanation, true parental alienation takes place when one parent intentionally influences the other child to behaviour negatively to the other parent in a horrible way. Although negative manner but does not mean there had being evidence of abusive, destructive or harmful parenting behaviours. One can only admit if the five common signs that a child is being affected by true parental alienation.

These are; the child's views towards the alienating parent to show as the good and honest parent which does not expresses only negative feelings toward the target parent but also ridicule him as bad parent. This ridiculing thinking will consistently have reinforced by the alienating parent until the child expresses hatred, contempt and fear regarding the target parent without not showing any guilt or remorse to worsen the situation. The child often denies being coached or influenced by one parent. Accusations and opinions of the alienating parent do insist that the child have to formulate ideas about the target parent on their own.

Another negativity that exists is the tension targeted parent is also extending to the extended family and therefore the child beginning to show signs of disobedience in their communication to the opposite parents. The direct and collateral damages may also result from parental alienation to long-lasting effects that are enormously destructive and destabilizing to both the children together with the parents involved.

Alienation affection and damages the child's sense of self and her ability to form lasting opinion, in relationships to their friends and family. The loss of connection of the alienated parent also damages the child's psychological thinking and understanding when it comes to her views, since she will now lack one parent as a role model without being able to benefit from that loss parent.

Parental alienation has such destructive long-term consequences for both parents and children, this extremely concerning that more is not being done by professionals to help the situation when early stage alienation happen to be taking place and take strategic actions to turn things around before it reaches critical and damaging stage. One unfortunate thing about child alienating is that, many courts and professionals who deal with cases are not trained to handle high-conflict divorce cases therefore they're unable to detect alienation at early stages where professional intervention could have the greatest impact of preventing the situation. Alienation is often hard to define or legally prove and many target parents trying to prove parental alienation in court which prove quite challenging, expensive and time-consuming.

Even if these parents are willing to do so, many of such court systems are not equipped to deal with such high-conflict parenting situations that need intensive intervention. In many occasion the courts systems are reluctant to deal with such cases or not even unable to effectively intervene in a consistently effective manner, for these parents are often find out that the family law attorneys cannot either minimize the situation and are reluctant to pursue the issues in court.

Many complicating cases cannot be followed up further, whence some parents refuse to participate in parent-child therapy and respond to guidance from a therapist and parenting coordinators unless it is ordered by the court and carefully monitored and evaluated on an on-going basis. In certain cases, the alienating parents usually use well-experienced litigation as a means to control the target parent, but many target parents are exhausted by cases of litigation and may fear that more legal intervention will only worsen the situation.

Parents seeking professional intervention truly understand the underlying dynamics of the problem before trying hard not to take the child's rejection personally but stay committed to positive co-parenting attitude. This also sometime advises parents to not give up hope despite the complexity of the situation. Because the journey to repair your relationship with your child involve can be long and often requires an enormous amount of patience and persistence. Child relationships sometimes it may take years before you will see the results of your choices and effort. Always think positive and never ever make the mistake of thinking you can do everything when it comes to the matter of your children's behaviour towards you. You can be more experience of these signs but it can turn to a strategy in which you can't help it any longer. Divorce Management Coach provides at Moving Forward in many occasions yet Divorce provides guidance to women and men as they learn how to manage the chaos that comes after the divorce. Combination of experiences such as a Family Law Paralegal which provides coaching and Training to clients with the resources, skills and strategies they need to save time, money and avoid headaches as they navigate through divorce. There are programs to learn about what harms children of divorce the most endure. Many affordable divorce coaching program, and Divorce seminars also includes a track devoted to parenting after divorce.

These are sufficient information on which to form an opinion. The way of your parenting time or contact between parenting circumstances of your divorce and your child's character could all play into evil's den. If the child tries to stay with you mean she will be going to miss some play dates with her friends and may wish she didn't have come to you. At the same time not want to tell you that because she doesn't want to hurt your feelings. He may not next time, want to come until she's settled down and happy and then have the conversation with you by reassuring her that she can be honest with you, that you're concerned about her well-being. Ask open questions and be sure not to paraphrase them to make her feel she has to choose or speak against the other parent. There is one tiny voice that silenced anyone who still had doubts that parental alienation is real and one of the most insidious forms of child abuse.

A boy openly made up his mind and lied about his father concerning his step-mother and threw himself widely opened to criticism some years back when the father was away working for the betterment him and his sideling. But his case was brought up at his father's divorce case where they were to meet for settlement by his devastated mother who has endured a 12-year court battle with her ex-husband to try to win back the heart and mind of their son.

This child has been one tiny soldier in the growing army of bitter children who are becoming collateral damage in bitter battles between ex-spouses that are overwhelming in Africa divorce courts, the first of its kind Symposium for Parental Alienation Syndrome (PAS) heard during these battles in Ghana.

Over some years had four different lawyers trying to convince the courts of a son who lived less than few hours' flight from the father who needed to see the mother who loved and raised him which was told to the conference.

It is sometime a believed that no parent would wound their child for their own selfish gain. But people still believe that losing your parent is not all that big a deal because you can lose your parents when they get old or when they get sick or even get car accidents and die. But alienated parents aren't dead but are alive which the children know it.

According to Grace's father it was her ex-girlfriend who began a fears campaign to solely seal the custody of their then 14-year old son and cut off all communication links to the father by his mother both physically and psychologically, shortly after the couple separated in 2001.

For PAS children generally there are no tangible signs of maltreatment by both sides but it is kidnapping of the mind which normally term as A Heart-breaking Story of Parental Alienation Syndrome.

Parental Alienation Syndrome has everything to do with who has custody of the said child. It's an idling calculated opportunity that are always argued against each parent in a battle to gain what have been produce by the two people whether is a syndrome or a mental health disorder or abuse just ties everyone up in knots while real children and real families suffer this strategy. What is usually seen as child's fundamental right to be loved by both his and her parents is rather destroyed by such wicked and cruelty by both parents just by lack of understanding.

The effects are long-lasting as far as both parents do not subside in their alienation ventures and are always doing more just to win the argument.

Adults who were alienated when they were children revealed that lifelong battles with low self-esteem, alcoholism and drug abuse, as well as high bad behaviour and fail in academic ventures

Parental alienation can to be known as malicious mother Dilemma but it's become opportunity form of emotional abuse of children over the last two decades, owning to a new study of some the growing trend cases in recent history of our world.

In 2001 when our struggle of child custody started it was seen among high-conflict divorce cases examined which has crippled families. Generally, women turned their kids against their father, while so many of the cases involved women alienating the kids against their fathers.

African family courts have decided to deal contentiously with divorces cases by awarding sole custody to one parent, believing that joint custody is simply unworkable among most African partners who are at war.

Most divorce experts including mental health professionals and child advocacy workers, some of them take the fight to conferences, have long argued that this approach encourages parental alienation by treating the children as prizes to be won or lost in bitter battle.

The only results confirmed in the usual divorce laws needed to be amended to make equal shared parenting a norm in all divorce cases, except strange circumstances such as domestic violence, mental health or other issues that will make the other parent clearly unfit.

In a case where the alienated parents is non-custodial fathers to engage those fathers is a significant challenge which sometimes one can be seen as the opposite individual who is not fit by lack of emanating from two sources the characteristics of men and fathers themselves. Traditional Patterns of gender-equality role can also direct men toward self-sufficiency and control independent problem-solving and emotional restraint to have largely worked against fathers being unable to acknowledge their short comings and ask for help. For the fear of self-disclosure and a feeling of disloyalty to their family to expose these families' problems is common fear of losing control over their life and the need to present an image of control. In the form of exterior calm, strength, and rationality, despite considerable inner turmoil which usually characterizes many fathers they try to maintain their position. Professional service providers also do not always consider such psychological obstacles to therapy and thus do not address fathers' unique needs. The research on divorced fathers shows clearly about their most pressing need of their continued meaningfully involvement with their children, as active parents. The lack of recognition of this primary need is the main reason why most professional's lack of success in engaging alienated fathers.

Pertaining to the key to engaging alienated parents is to validate their parental identity, and combine advocacy efforts with counselling to focus on enhancing their role as active and responsible father. Professionals who for recently have been notably seen dangers of absentee father in the politics of reform with respect to the issue of legal child custody which the society are desperately indeed of as allies in policy reform efforts. The greatest important role of human service professionals should be supporting alienated parents through such advocacy and activisms, challenging the custodial and non-custodial residential parent duties are to advancing the cause of co-parenting.

An active program to educate an individual on this subject is essential as alienated parents report lack this effective support services and therefore remain a highly vulnerable population. Professional service providers need to be persistent and proactive and take time to build and sustain engagement in the context of these parents' feelings of isolation, helplessness, and their tendency to wait until there is a crisis before accessing support. Parents who were highly involved with are attached to their children and suddenly find themselves forcefully removed from their children's lives experience profound wontedness. Those parents who are experiencing of being removed from loving parent life of one's child by a sole custody order strikes the heart of many individual fathers. These sees suicide rates reports at epidemic proportions among such parents fathers in particular, who always struggling to maintain a parenting relationship with their children legal abuse as a key factor in these cases. Being vigilant regarding symptoms of post-traumatic stress and suicidal ideation among non-custodial and alienated fathers and mothers is an essential role for professional service providers. A struggling-based approach is by the way of recognizing alienated parent's aspirations to their children's wellbeing specially to impart experience, knowledge and skills that they can contribute to this welfare of the child while addressing the alienation problems.

There are many areas of concern for social workers working with divorced or separated couples with children who are facing the problems of parental alienation. Their efforts on these parents are to turn a child who may be against the other parent, and parental alienation syndrome, or a child's unwarranted rejection of one parent in response to the attitudes and actions of the other parent. Social workers will encounter these problems in a number of ways, such as family service agencies, schools, and family court, as well as private practice working with high-conflict divorcing couples. These parents who believe that the other parent has or will turn the children against them as alienated children will refuse to see such a parent, adults who are still alienated from a parent or elders who have lost their children battle to parental alienation.

Some social workers may be unaware of the name Parental Alienation Syndrome for this particular problem yet they have probably dealt with it over the course of their careers. For example, individual clients may enter individual counselling therapy to solve the problem of depression, or relationship problems and later reveal that they have been cut off from one parent by another parent. These clients may be unaware of the meaning of the lost relationship and may even minimize its effect on their development, and current mental health concerns.

Children academic record in school or in the society may prompt the social workers casually reveal that they have no contact with a hated parent. When questioned about the absent parent, these children may vehemently denounce the parent as bad and rubbish. The parents of such a child may be manoeuvring behind the scenes to exclude the other parent from the child's school life by misrepresenting that parent's intentions to school staff, withholding information from that parent to create the appearance of a lack of interest, and removing contact information from school records. Another scenario the represented clients who enter therapy counselling is consumed with fear that the other parent is turning the children against them. Such parents will be desperate for advice and guidance about how to cope with the provocation of the other parent. These parents live with anxiety, depression, and helplessness, as well as feelings of victimization by the other parents. The children and the legal systems deals with legal and mental health issues that is not always responsive to the needs of targeted parents.

In such cases social workers may formulate ways that will defined the other one parent and engineer the child's rejection of the other parent. But unless the social worker is familiar with parental alienation as an act of parental alienation syndrome, he or she may be missing useful information for understanding how one parent is able to poison a child's relationship with the other parent in the absence of just cause.

Child Custody struggle is known as Parental alienation and it is a strategy that a parent uses to undermine and to foster a child's rejection of the other parent. Parental alienation syndrome in not new in the developed world, It develops in children who come to hate, fear, and reject the targeted parent as someone unworthy of having caring heart to coined the other children to hate the other parent known as Parental alienation syndrome as already described.

How a mother will campaign against her Divorce husband to gain access to her children.
Children are engulfing with hatred of the targeted parent that leads to alienating. They do not remember any positive past experiences with such father only to reject all contact and communication to satisfy the alienator. Men who once loved and valued his children overnight has become hated and feared.

If you ask the alienated children about the reasons for their intense hostility toward the targeted parent they cannot offer any better explanations to the magnitude that typically to the rejection that parent. Some of these children may complain about the parent's eating habits, food preparation or their caring attitude some also make wild accusations that turns out possibly be true. These affected alienated children exhibit a lack of affection of their alienated parent and therefore demonstrating an automatic hatred and dislike to support their action. The alienator parent is perceived as perfect while the father is also seen as useless in his effort to win the once loved child like him again. If an alienated child is asked to identify any bad thing the alienated father has done that justify negative aspect of the alienating parent probably draw a negative utterances. These show the fact that most children have mixed feelings about even the best parents they may have.

There are many different ways to confirm that one has been manipulated by a parent to unnecessarily reject the other parent and what region catalysts the other parent to represents both good and bad news of the other. We have good news that many ways families adapted to resolve from alienation to realization. But there is no magic to reach this process only if one is willing to sort peace through this channel. Even though some affected parents have their own way of doing it is a matter of time before one will gain experience. Others use the alienating parent as an example being alienated by someone turning on them and, for others; it is becoming a parent being the target of parental alienating from their own children.

There are a few cases that are sore, resulting from the either the father will take a horrible discussion that may end the lives of the family together or may kill himself from such useless situation. Sometimes things slowly chip itself away from of a long-held belief system, which awaken a different truth and a more authentic. Such gained self-respect connection to reality may be grateful to know the truth. This self-acknowledgement that turns this truth is hard be won and quite painful. Once the parents are aware of the parental alienation, they had to come to terms with this painful truth that the alienating parent did not have their best interest at heart, these children they have, probably behaved very differently toward someone like them who did not deserve such treatment, and that they missed out on a relationship that may have real value and benefit to their life.

It May be probably surprising, that adult children who have parental alienation syndrome believed that the experience will have negative long-term consequences on their life but are unable to find solution to such problem. Many says they're suffering from depression and therefore turn to drugs and alcohol to quench their pain, but failed relationships and multiple divorces most sadly, becoming alienated from their own children later in life. These are the ways, the intergenerational cycle of parental alienation syndrome as perpetuated.

These are some Alienation Tactics.

Some of the adult children with parental alienation syndrome devise a wild range of alienating strategies, including constant bad behaviour against the[r targeted parent, chronic interference with visitation, communication, and emotional manipulation to choose one parent over the other. There had been more than 1,300 specific actions to describe these. There had been a considerable attempts complete overlap in the strategies identified by the targeted parents with those described by adult children.

What are the problems working with Targeted Parents

Professionals workers counselling parents who are facing parental alienation who need support, education, and guidance suffer allot. Such worker's primary role is to help their client about parental alienating what primary behaviours that a child will display against the other parent and parental alienation syndrome what that behavioural manifestations of an alienated child so the parent can determine the facts about the problem. These clients must be encouraged to look at themselves and their relationship with their children prior to blaming the other parent for their difficulties.

The conclusions will be that parental alienation may work against the targeted parent and therefore should be taught a series of responses to prevent parental alienation. This can allow the targeted parent to maintain the highest behaviour not becoming overly passive or reactive. The greatest possible thing such parents need is daily validation and support in dealing with the pain and suffering associated with parental alienation.

Another way is working With Alienated Children
Professional Social workers who volunteer help children currently who are alienated must be self-reflective in other words an example to follow and be aware so that they do not collide with the child against the targeted parent. A second concern is to avoid becoming intimidated or manipulated by the alienating parent also against their target. The child should learn to develop critical thinking skills in order to help him or her ability to resist the pressure to choose to move away from this behaviour. The affected child's attitude to targeted parent and their relationship to that parent must be validated for the child to advice the child of his or her next step. Such worker can be a role model who values and respects the targeted parent in order to counter the behaviour message that this parent should discard, private practitioners family service agencies or school settings, social workers who are working with clients affected should be able to help the parental alienation victims. Some of these individuals may even be unaware of the source of such pain and suffering or uninformed about the name and nature of this phenomenon. Familiarity on the worker is the first step to provide the client with better information, guidance, and hope when dealing with this complicated and painful issue like this. Nothing stirs up controversy more than the controversy generated when parents are at war over the custody of a child.

Controversies are an issue where evidence on both sides can make a compelling case. It may never be polarized whether black and white, but when people have their emotions flare up on an issue it can quickly turn into two polar opposites.

Fairness takes over reasoning, incomplete facts become evidence, and court schedules become complicated with repeated visits to a judge to try to bring sanity to whoever is unlikely to ever be insane. One thing to beware of is social movements who may be promoting one side over another in their feeble justice. The court maintains pass laws to bring order to chaos but when Gender wars are fuelled lives are destroyed.

How I became exposure to custody wars stems from Social parental show from United Kingdom where Parent fight bitterly over their kids every day. Many of these parents in such gathering show classes were litigating over child custody. In such motion shows most wanted to settle the case, but none of them would like to give access of the child to the other which seemed to be the only alternative open to them for settlement.

It was quiet disturbing to see that in such many cases, the child will behave outrageously, to the point of cursing their parents, even kick, spit on them and calls them stupid, a horrible thing that usually happens. All people will be sitting unconcern because no one can help them out of such terrible situation unless they come to their senses of the damage being cause to their child. What can you or one do when the children are caught up in such a fight and starts taking sides I came to realize that at such a level of conflict in custody disputes the fallout is from sweeping societal changes around in our society?

When can these changes help to shape the society?

Since the end of the 1970's, women have taken more active role in going to work and going back to college to pursue careers as never before. This shift has bought many changes to our society and became more women getting involved in the day-to-day carrier building more than what it was truly in previous generations. The complications are when parental roles began to fall apart, than the *tender years* where the parental doctrine was still in place. As our religious doctrine still convict us that by virtue of the fact that a women is the keeper of the home as the mother of our kids. Couples were the mother of our children that they must be the superior parents. In the early 1970's several coutries obey the no fault divorce laws, where anyone who wanted out of a marriage was free to leave. Some have called it the no guilt laws. There was a proliferation of divorce that was historically unprecedented.

After a family breakup, many fathers wanted to continue to be involved with the care of their children. Suddenly, they found that they had no legal right to have custody of their children unless the mother agreed to it.

Due to the lobbying efforts of James Cook, founder of the Joint Custody Association, who was caught up in this problem himself, this made California legislature s passed the first joint custody laws.

Joint custody was widely seen as a better way of handling this problem by evolving both parents to share child custody equally. It was then perceived that would lead to fewer fights over the custody of children because it was more equal opportunity for both parents. These followed by other states in United State also passed joint custody laws that allow both parents to enjoy their children presence every day equally. These laws helped to bring peace as is seen as level the playing field for fathers.

The most mothers and fathers welcomed joint custody as fair. Others even don't want to see the children's father come in contact with them. There was backlash since child custody become highly sensitive issue with the ramping up of high-level disputes ever since the changes in our society. In most countries the tender years of the child's years is presumed as the mother knows best has been replaced with the best interests for the child as joint custody which is seen as the best for both parents.

In the beginning of 1980's, the Law began to increasingly ignore gender in determining child custody. This removed the automatic full custody rights to the mother and these lead to having less time with their children. Instead the Law looked first at how the custody could be shared but if that is seen as impossible the judicial officers attempted to determine which parent was more interested and better able to attend to the best interest of the child.

This Lead the Fathers perceived that they were at risk of disadvantage because of bias toward the mother having permanent custody rights. Because of this more fathers than never showing up at parenting classes to make sure that their skills also can make a difference. This made the Authorises take up the issues and paid attention to its contents.

Most parents were able to share custody of their children, and they worked out childcare issues in an amicable.

A large number of women were even relieved to have fathers share in the childcare, which enabled them to pursue their personal life goals in their educational career.

However, when the atmosphere became unfriendly to resolve child custody the fathers found themselves that they have greater opportunity to gain joint or primary custodial status by going to court. The issue got even higher when the legal system was used to resolve these difficult problems evenly. In most hard cases, the alienation of a child's affection against a targeted parent became a bizarre escalation of the intensity of more conflict.

Who discovered Parental Alienation Syndrome (PAS)?

With growing child-custody cases forensic psychiatrist Dr. Richard A. Gardner first identified Parental Alienation Syndrome in the 1980's. He noticed that the issue need to be addressed as dramatic increase in the frequency of child custody disorder rarely as observed before the programming of brainwashing of a child by one parent to alienate the other parent.

However, the disorder wasn't just brainwashing or programming by a parent. It was a serious founded issue that Dr. Gardner calls it self-created contributions by the child in support of the alienating parent's campaign of denigration against the targeted parent. He called this disorder Parental Alienation Syndrome (PAS), a new term that includes the contribution to the problem made by both the parent and the child. He defines it as follows;

1. The Parental Alienation Syndrome is a disorder that arises primarily in the context of child-custody disputes.

2. Its primary manifestation is the child's campaign of denigration against a parent, a campaign that has no justification.

3. It results from the combination of brainwashing of a parent's indoctrinations and the child's own contributions to the vilification of the targeted parent. This extract is from: Gardner, R.A. (1998). The Parental Alienation Syndrome, Second Edition, Cresskill, NJ: Creative Therapeutics, Inc.

These are the child's contribution to the part in PAS

Gardner notes that the PAS is more than brainwashing or programming, because the child has to actually participate in the denigrating of the alienated parent. This is done in primarily the following eight ways:

1. The child denigrates the alienated parent with abusive language and severe oppositional behaviour.
2. The child usually offers weak, absurd, or frivolous reasons for his or her anger.
3. The child will be sure of himself or herself and doesn't demonstrate i.e. love and hate for the alienated parent, only hate.
4. The child will come up with ideas of denigration. This phenomenon is where the child asserts that no one told him to do this.
5. The child supports professional feels that there should be a need to protect the alienating parent.
6. The child always does not demonstrate guilt over cruelty towards their alienated parent.
7. The child uses borrowed words scenarios to describe the situations or she could not have experienced.
8. The situation is sometimes spread to the friends and extended family of the alienated parent.

In severe cases of parent alienation, the child is utterly brain- washed against the alienated parent. The alienator can truthfully say that the child doesn't want to spend any time with the other parent even though he or she has mighty secure court injunction. The alienator typically will say there isn't anything that I can do about it. I'm not telling him not to see you.

PAS is an escalation part of Parental Alienation which Dr. Douglas Darnall in his book Divorce Casualties: Protecting Your Children from Parental Alienation describes three categories of PA:

These are mild categories which he calls it's the naïve alienators. They are ignorant of damage they cause to the child and they need to be educated and change.

The moderate once are the active alienators. When they are triggered, they lose control of appropriate boundaries. They use their abusive languages and when they calm down, they don't want to admit that they were out of control.

The severe categories are the obsessed alienators or those who are involved in parental alienation syndrome. They operate from a delusional system where every cell of their body committed to destroying the other parent's relationship with the child. His latter case, he wrote that we don't have an effective protocol for treating obsessed alienators other than removing the child from their influence.

The important point in Parental Alienating Syndrome is that no true parental abuse and neglect on the part of the alienated parent. If it is true in each case, the child's animosity would be justified. In other way Parental Alienating Syndrome is not that the child still has a positive relationship with the parent, even though one parent is attempting to alienate the child from him or her.

According to most likely to initiate Parental Alienating Syndrome cases Gardner's statistics showed that the majority of PAS occurrences are initiated by mothers. Mothers have traditionally had primary custody of the children before the 20th century Law which favour both parents, but the mothers usually want to spend more time with their children.

In order to advert alienating of a child one parent needs to have considerable time with the child. However, in recent years increasing numbers of fathers have started instigating Parental Alienating Syndrome, since there are no strong Laws or legal sanctions for doing so.

There are a few cases where the fathers were seen as the alienators.

In one case, the father had no control over his obsession to trash the mother.

Numerous professionals told him, including the mother, that he could have shared custody if he would be willing to follow the rules. He didn't have the self-control to do this.

When he lost custody because of his aberrant behaviour, he became a celebrity in the father's rights movement and took his campaign into national circles. No one would know from hearing him speak about his situation that there was serious pathology going on (PAS) or how hard the professionals worked to stabilize it.

Moreover, in cultures where women traditionally have no tangible rights, alienation by the father can be severe.

I've met divorcing women who had been prevented from learning how to make a living to support themselves. At the time of separation all access to financial resources were stopped and the children removed from her care. These women reported severe alienation of affection.

It makes one grateful to have laws that protect human rights and enforce a better way of resolving conflict than a winner-take all approach.

How common is PA and PAS?

When parents first separate there is often parent alienation. For example, due to the anxiety of the mother, she is likely to say indirectly to a child that he or she is not safe with the father.

She might say:

"Call me as soon as you get there to let me know you are okay."
"If you get scared, you call me right away. Okay?"
"I'll come get you if you want to come home."

Usually this level of alienation dies down after the separating parents get used to changes brought on by the separation and move on with their lives.

However, in rare cases, the anxiety not only doesn't calm down, it escalates. PAS parents are psychologically fragile. When things are going their way, they can hold themselves together. When they are threatened however, they can become fiercely entrenched in preserving what they see is rightfully theirs.

Fortunately, only a small percentage end up in this level of conflict.

Why do PAS parents act like they do?

I believe that PAS parents have become stuck in the first stage of child development, where survival skills are learned.

To them, having total control over their child is a life and death matter. Because they don't understand how to please other people, any effort to do so always has strings attached. They don't give; they only know how to take. They don't play by the rules and are not likely to obey a court order.

Descriptions that are commonly used to describe severe cases of PAS are that the alienating parent is unable to "individuate" (a psychological term used when the person is unable to see the child as a separate human being from him or herself). They are often described as being "overly involved with the child" or "enmeshed".

The parent may be diagnosed as narcissistic (self-centred), where they presume that they have a special entitlement to whatever they want. They think that there are rules in life, but only for other people, not for them.

Also, they may be called a sociopath, which means a person who has no moral conscience. These are people who are unable to have empathy or compassion for others. They are unable to see a situation from another person's point of view, especially their child's point of view. They don't distinguish between telling the truth and lying in the way that others do.

In spite of admonitions from judges and mental health professionals to stop their alienation, they can't. The prognosis for severely alienating parents is very poor. It is unlikely that they are able to "get it." It is also unlikely that they will ever stop trying to perpetuate the alienation. This is a gut wrenching survival issue to them.

How does the child get involved in PAS?

The targeted parent needs to understand what has happened to what as once an affectionate and loving child who is now unexplainably hostile. Remember Gardner's definition stated earlier, "the disorder wasn't only brainwashing or programming by a parent, but was confounded by what he calls *self-created contributions by the child in support of the alienating parent's campaign of denigration against the targeted parent*." It isn't PAS in the severe form of this disorder, unless the child has crossed over and joined up with the alienating parent. The child shares the alienating parent's psychosis. How does this happen?

At birth, children are totally reliant on a parent, usually the mother, for having all of their needs met. It is part of normal child development to be enmeshed with their primary caregiver, and very young children do not have a separate identity from this caregiver.

One of the mother's roles is to help the child develop as a separate person, therefore, infancy and childhood become a series of tasks of learning how to become independent. For example, learning to putting oneself back to sleep, eating, toilet training and caring for one's hygiene.

Instead of promoting this independence, the alienating parent encourages continued dependence. The parent may insist on sleeping with the child, feeding the child ("It's easier if I do it"), and taking care of these rites of passage longer than normal child development calls for. This "spoiling" may not feel right to the child, but they do not have enough ego strength to do anything about it.

A PAS mother can't imagine that the father is capable of planning the child's time while in his care. Therefore, she arranges several things for the child to do while at the father's house. One of the most common ways of doing this is to sign the child up for on-going lessons without permission from the father.

The parent may even decree whom the child can and cannot see, particularly specific members of the child's extended family on the father's side. The mother desperately wants control over the time when the child isn't with her.

One of the most unusual situations that I ran into was the father who picked up his sons at 9:00 a.m. on a Saturday for the weekend. He discovered that his very excited boys had their hearts set on going to Disneyland for the day, when this idea had never crossed his mind.

One theory about why a mother will act this way is that when a father takes his share of joint custody, it is like asking her to give away part of her body. One mother said, "He is going to remove my right arm and take it for the weekend." It feels like the mother has lost a profound part of who she is as a person. She feels fractured, pulled apart.

Why is PAS a double bind for the child?

When children spend time with the father, and enjoy it, they are put into a double bind. Clearly, they cannot tell the mother that dad treats them well or that they had fun together. They want to bond with the father, but don't dare. They figure out on which side the bread is buttered (who has the power), and their survival needs tug at them. Therefore, children will tell the mother about everything they didn't enjoy about time spent with the father, which will add to her belief that they don't like to be with him. These children feel that they must protect the mother. The same is true when the alienator is the father. The child will avoid expressing their affectionate feelings for the mother to him.

Family volatility

These are volatile families. The father may have indeed spanked a child, or lashed out at the mother physically or emotionally. An isolated incidence can turn into a holocaust. One father spanked his rebellious child and ended up in jail on child abuse charges, followed by a six week trial to determine his guilt. The jury returned with a not guilty verdict in 20 minutes. The verdict didn't end it as far as the mother was concerned, however.

The alienating parent's hatred can have no bounds. The severest form will bring out every horrible allegation known, including claims of domestic violence, stalking and the sexual molestation of the child. Many fathers say that there have been repeated calls to the Department of Family and Child Services alleging child abuse and neglect.

In most cases the investigators report that they found nothing wrong. However, the indoctrinating parent feels that these reports are not fabrications, but very, very real. She can describe the horror of what happen in great detail. Regardless of the actual truth, in her mind, it did happen.

Most of the alienated fathers that I work with are continually befuddled by her lying. "How can she lie like that?" They don't realize that these lies are not based on rational thinking. They are incapable of understanding the difference between what is true and what they want to be true. A vital part of fighting PAS is to understand the severity of the psychological disturbance that is the source of it.

Intergenerational patterns

What makes this problem very complicated is that PAS is often intergenerational in dysfunctional families. Almost always the alienator has people within the family who support the alienation. It might be the mother, father or grandparent who encourage fighting. They are likely to support the parent financially or even provide massive amounts of money to fund litigation.

This is further proof to the PAS parent that he or she is justified in what he/she does.

When a child is placed in the role of the parent's therapist

Alienation advances even further when the alienating parent uses the child as a personal therapist. The child is told about every miserable experience and negative feeling about the alienated parent with great specificity. The child, who is already enmeshed with the parent because his or her own identity is still undefined, easily absorbs the parent's negativity. They become aligned with this parent and feel that they need to be the protector of the alienating parent.

What happens to the child when you can't stop PAS?

Obviously, without anyone to stop the alienation from progressing, the child will become estranged from the alienated parent. The relationship with this parent will eventually be severed. It is doubtful that, without psychological intervention as the child grows, he or she will ever understand what happened.

The child's primary role model will be the maladaptive, dysfunctional parent. He or she will not have the benefit of growing up with the most well-adjusted parent and all that this parent can contribute to enrich the child's life. Many of these children come to experience serious psychiatric problems.

Will they ever grow up and realize what happened to them? Without someone who can recognize the syndrome and counsel them about it, it isn't likely that they will ever figure it out. However, there have been exceptions where the child and the alienated parent have been successfully reunified later in life.

How can good intentions backfire?

Those people who are typically called upon to handle such difficult situations, such as the police, social workers, attorneys or psychologists assume that what the frightened mother is saying is true. These things DO happen. There are men who are seriously disturbed, violent, out of control sexually, and stalk, who are rightfully feared. The mother is very convincing in her desperation and vivid in her descriptions. The clincher is that the alienated child collaborates with the mother by saying, "Yes, I am afraid of my father." "Yes, my father did touch me down there." "Yes, he does beat me." What would you do if you were faced with having to decide how to protect a child in such a situation?

Therapists

Some therapists don't realize the severity and depth of the problem. In fact, they may unwittingly side with the alienating parent and even testify in court that the child is afraid of the alienated parent. This can be a serious stumbling block in getting an accurate diagnosis. Indeed, it can tip the scale into the alienating parent's agenda and do real damage.

Our courts, social services and mental health workers are all committed to stop child abuse and neglect when they see it occurring. Unfortunately, in PAS situations a dramatic and loud complaint from the alienating parent often ends up being acted upon without an investigation as to the accuracy of the allegation. This frequently removes the alienated parent from the children and allows the alienating parent considerable additional time to proceed with the alienation.

By the time all of the evaluations are in place and the case is heard by the court, considerable damage has been done to the child. It is an irony that the very people we turn to for help in such a difficult situation can often be those who most contribute to allowing the on-going abuse and neglect of the child to continue.

What can be done about the problem?

First, it takes a sophisticated mental health professional to be able to identify that PAS is occurring. Most forensic evaluators such as psychiatrists and clinical psychologists have studied the disorder and are able to recognize it.

Forensic evaluators diagnose PAS by having the parents take a battery of psychological tests, doing a detailed case history and by observation. They make recommendations as to what to do. After the evaluator has written a report on the family and made recommendations, nothing will happen to resolve the crisis without court intervention.

The alienated parent has to take the report to a judge who must then be convinced that the child is being alienated and that it is not in their best interest to stay in such an environment.

It is rare however that judges have any degree of mental health training. They most often learn about PAS from the bench. It usually takes several trips to court to point out how badly a child is being treated before a judge is willing to act.

How are PAS cases resolved legally?

Judges are inevitably conservative in their orders. Even when the evidence is overwhelming that the alienation is occurring, the court order may still end up saying, "the parents are to make joint decisions about the child's welfare," when this is impossible to do.

This is further evidence that the judge doesn't understand the magnitude of the problem. The judge in one of the most severe PAS cases I worked on was from the old school. He was tired of having the litigants continue to appear before him. One day he said, "Why don't the two of you go out in the hallway and kiss and make up." This is an example of how frustrating these cases are for judges. Indeed, these are the hardest cases to decide.

Judges have been slow to place serious sanctions on the alienating parent. If there is no threat of severe fines, jail time or sole custody to the targeted parent, the chances are remote that the out-of-control parent can be stopped.

It usually takes a dramatic situation where court orders are broken to force the court to change primary custody. Often it is only a matter of time before alienating parents become desperate and their unstable mental health gets the better of them. People in an official position start to recognize the alienating parent as being out of line, and become supportive of the targeted parent.

In one case, the 9 and 4 year old daughters were abducted and presumed to be on their way to Australia through an underground group that hides women who are victims of domestic violence, often of a sexual nature and where the father is stalking. The girls were missing for 3 months and found in another county where they were waiting for final arrangements to be made before their departure. When the police broke into the house at 3:00 a.m., they found the girls sleeping with their mother. They had been given boy's names, clothes, haircuts and their hair was dyed. They were not allowed contact with anyone outside of their hiding place, not even to go to school. The oldest child had strep throat and the youngest was seriously withdrawn.

In another case, the mother could no longer convince the social workers, the police or the Court about her allegations. She was known to be unstable because she had "cried wolf" too many times. She abducted her daughter to Utah. She told officials there that the courts where she lived were protecting a proven child molester. The press was called. After she was interviewed; there was a virtual feeding frenzy as the father's photograph and the story was on all the local news networks.

A big part of the problem was that the seven year old girl, said "Yes" when asked if her father had molested her. Even though this had already been disproved by forensic evaluators, she was still confused.

Can the alienation of children be reversed?
As children get older, the alienation can be reversed with proper psychological care. However, it won't work if the alienating parent is not contained. In the last case described above, the mother had severely limited visiting rights. She had remarried and had a new child; however, she still regularly calls the police to report the father for abuse. Presently, the daughter resides with her father, receives weekly therapy and hates the police. She gradually understands how disturbed her mother is In the former case, where the mother was kidnapping the

I fought this battle for about five years and walked away last year. I am happier now than I was then and expect to be even more so next year at this time. My four were/are teens and young adults. I was always so deeply hurt by the disgust, contempt and disdain, while their father walked on water. He who had rarely made it home in time to join us for dinner, he who was not taking them to gymnastics classes, swimming lessons, camps, dr appts, etc while they were growing up. It is very sad because I can see how he is using them and manipulating them with promises of hefty life insurance. They all still live with him! - I suspect they will for a long time since he is too lonely to allow them a way to move out. Instead, some of them have boy and girlfriends who have moved in as well. Our youngest daughter - in high school - is easily manipulated and he uses her for backrubs and other physical things I would consider to be inappropriate. Remember though, he is a saint and I am the worst parent on the planet. I don't see her or any of them as victims - he is their choice for parent of the year.I merely exited the stage and let them enjoy their choice.I have a wonderful few dogs who are more deserving of my time and affection. My teen and young adult children actually saved me a great deal of money by pushing me out of their lives. And there is some relief to do it early on in their lives as well. I won't know any grandchildren since I am out of their lives before any are born, I won't be second place at any weddings as I was at the Scouting and high school graduation ceremonies/events, and I am nearly completely free of their hatred, as well as the sadness and despair that felt so overwhelming last year at this time.

I can admire those of you willing to stick it out but I am just not seeing any change down the road. My Chihuahua has an entire wardrobe and will never turn on me like my children did. I will be fine. I hope they have nice lives

My partner's son packed up a left our home about a month ago while we were not home. It was a total shock for us as he did not spend much time at his mother's. He left a note in his bedroom saying that he was very stressed and that we had too high expectations for him but at the end said that he still loved him as his father. After he left we only talked to him a few times as he was avoiding us but now he will not talk to us at all nor any of my partner's family. We are all shocked and this is soo unlike him and we are all very concerned for him. My partner does believe that his ex has talked about him very poorly in front of the kids (two boys) since the separation (which was over approximately 8 or more years ago) and even showed them court documents after a 50/50 custody agreement. She even took her son to court with her at one point. I'm sure she had said and done many more things but just giving you idea of the type of things she had done. It is heart breaking as these kids have been in my life now over 5 years and I treat them like my own. I don't understand how she can be so selfish and not realize the damage that she is doing to her children's mental health. What is even more frustrating is that myself and my partner feel like there is absolutely nothing we can do to prevent this or help his son. The other son is following the 50/50 custody agreement of a week with us and a week with his mother and he seems to be doing fine. We have been asking him some questions but not too many as he seems to not want to get involved (like rat on his mother.) Anyways hope to get some advice here on this situation and if there are any other avenues we can take to help

I'm a 57 year old mom of 3 daughters that I raised. I was their class moms, girl scout leaders, soccer moms, dance mom, all while holding down a full time job. They were 3,6 and 8 when we divorced. He was a decent guy back then, just not a good husband and we divorced amicably. A year later he began dating his 2nd wife. I saw a change in the way he treated me. And I heard from the kids there was lots of mom bashing taking place. I told the girls to let it "go in one ear and out the other". I tried to talk to him about it but I no longer recognized who he was. So I would respond with answers, when the kids came home angry, like "do you live with them? Then don't worry about it." or "Isn't it sad they have nothing else to talk about?" I truly thought he was damaging his relationship with his kids. Fast forward 15 years and they are 19, 22 and 24. I only have a relationship with my 19 yr old. The other two never see me, one hates me and the oldest has no feelings for me whatsoever. I often wish I was dead. I know I was a good and loving mother, they all had huge scholarships to top colleges and were overachievers. My 22 yr old is fighting for her life - stage 4 lymphoma bone cancer. And she still won't have anything to do with me. She has not spoken to me in 3 years when she had "an opportunity to be closer to her father" and when I asked her to put our differences aside (I never understood what they were, she just came home from college her sophomore year and hated me, after we were so close while she was growing up) during her war on cancer. She said no. She blames me for being misdiagnosed twice while in her father's care, I didn't even know anything about it. My 24 yr old only contacts me to tell me to leave my 22 year old alone. In all my life I never thought this was possible. I have a relationship with my youngest which I am eternally grateful for but it doesn't take away from the agony of not having my other daughter's in my life. I am also fighting cancer, malt lymphoma in my stomach. But not nearly as serious as my daughters. I don't know how to go on, I just get up every day and put one-foot in front of the other. But in all honestly, the desire to live has gone right out the window. I feel all I do is cry. How could this happen? I feel like I've been in a nightmare the last 3 years there is no waking up from. To date, through my daughter's brain surgery to her diagnosis, her father has not once contacted me. It's like he just wiped me out of their lives, in his mind

Gardner described PAS as a preoccupation by the child with criticism and deprecation of a parent.[20] Gardner stated that PAS occurs when, in the context of child custody disputes, one parent deliberately or unconsciously attempts to alienate a child from the other parent.[21] According to Gardner, PAS is characterized by a cluster of eight symptoms that appear in the child. These include a campaign of denigration and hatred against the targeted parent; weak, absurd, or frivolous rationalizations for this deprecation and hatred; lack of the usual ambivalence about the targeted parent; strong assertions that the decision to reject the parent is theirs alone (the "independent-thinker phenomenon"); reflexive support of the favored parent in the conflict; lack of guilt over the treatment of the alienated parent; use of borrowed scenarios and phrases from the alienating parent; and the denigration not just of the targeted parent but also to that parent's extended family and friends.[13][18][22] Despite frequent citations of these factors in scientific literature, "the value ascribed to these factors has not been explored with professionals in the field."[23]

Gardner and others have divided PAS into mild, moderate and severe levels. The number and severity of the eight symptoms displayed increase through the different levels. The recommendations for management differ according to the severity level of the child's symptoms. While a diagnosis of PAS is made based on the child's symptoms, Gardner stated that any change in custody should be based primarily on the symptom level of the alienating parent.[24] In mild cases, there is some parental programming against the targeted parent, but little or no disruption of visitation, and Gardner did not recommend court-ordered visitation. In moderate cases, there is more parental programming and greater resistance to visits with the targeted parent. Gardner recommended that primary custody remain with the programming parent if the brainwashing was expected to be discontinued, but if not, that custody should be transferred to the targeted parent. In addition, therapy with the child to stop alienation and remediate the damaged relationship with the targeted parent was recommended. In severe cases, children display most or all of the 8 symptoms, and will refuse steadfastly to visit the targeted parent, including threatening to run away or commit suicide if the visitation is forced. Gardner recommended that the child be removed from the alienating parent's home into a transition home before moving into the home of the targeted parent. In addition, therapy for the child is recommended.[1][22][24] Gardner's proposed intervention for moderate and severe PAS, including court-ordered transfer to the alienated parent, fines, house arrest, incarceration, have been critiqued for their punitive nature towards the alienating parent and alienated child, and for the risk of abuse of power and violation of their civil rights.[25][26] With time, Gardner revised his views and expressed less support for the most aggressive management strategies.[25]

My husband (target) is at the beginning stages of parental alienation by his ex wife (alienator). My husband is father of three children with his ex, 7, 8 and 11. We have them every other day, take them to gymnastics and soccer every weekend, make it a point to maintain as dependable a schedule as possible, and always make time for bonding time. Our motto is "consistency" and "balance" for the kiddos. I would like to think that my husband and I do everything in our power to insure the kiddos are well balanced, healthy, and loved when they are with us. My husband is without a doubt the most loving, honest, and wonderful father I have been blessed to witness. He does everything for his kids.

Now for the point, my husbands ex was never on good terms with us. She was extremely jealous and hostile at the beginning of our relationship. Although she loves her kids, she often does not bath them, never seems to have time to do homework them, feeds them chicken nuggets for dinner and cupcakes for breakfast, often leaves the kids at her mothers to go out on days she is allegedly has them, etc. My husband recently went through his 11 yr. old son's phone to find frantic text messages to his mother asking her when she will be home, he does not feel safe at his grandmother's, and begging her to come home at 2am. He also discovered the fact that his ex will text his son about how his father called her and that his father is angry at him and her, and why did he tell his dad that she left them at their grandma's, etc. Essentially she does not keep their "co-parenting" conversations to herself and expresses arguments to the kids that they having. Painting a very hostile and false picture of my husband. In short, she is manipulating the kids to love her chaotic, materialistic, and unorganized world, making my husband out to be a tyrant of a father who abuses their mother verbally.

There are so many other things, I could write a book. My husband and I are at out wits end. We have noticed that the kids have been acting differently since she a new bf in the picture (who is a complete rude low life). They have been distant, cry when we go to pick them up from their mother's, fight tooth and nail over homework and bath, telling my husband that "mom is better", personally attacking each other over things they never used to, and count down the minutes until they go back to their mothers. It has taken a deep toll on my husband who cherishes every minute he has with the kids. I am not saying we are perfect but we live and breath for these kiddos and their mother showed a less than stellar performance in her mother duties for as long as I've known her. Why do the kids cling to her and reject us? It's beginning to break our hearts..

Any advice is greatly appreciated

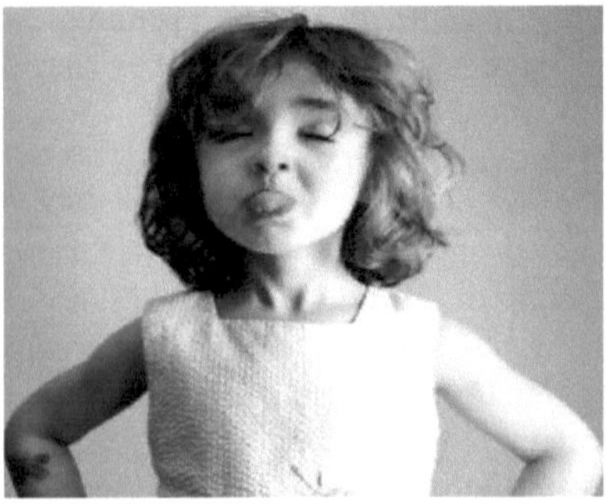

What do you want from am not coming with you?

Parental alienation occurs often, but not always, in the context of divorce and custody battles. No one knows how many children are exposed to parental alienation or show signs of the parental alienation syndrome, but we do know that it can happen to mothers as well as fathers, to custodial parents as well as non-custodial parents and to kids as young as toddlers or as old as teens. It is marked by sudden changes in your child's interactions with you and you'll see new personality traits begin to emerge.

Here are some attitudes and behaviours to watch for:

Leave me alone. Your child is filled with animosity toward you. When confronted and reminded of the good times you two once shared, she insists you two NEVER had a good relationship although you know that is not true. Suddenly, your once-loving and affectionate child seems to fear and, in some cases, despise you. He may even be reluctant to share a meal with you as though merely being in your presence is unbearable. When you question this, your child gives you frivolous and absurd reasons for this newfound negativity.

It's all your fault. Your child acts as if the other parent can do no wrong. Everything the other parent does is perfect in his eyes something your child never seemed to feel about your ex during the marriage. Your child seems to forgive your ex even the most inexcusable behaviour while ridiculing you for minor flaws and infractions.

Yeah, what he said. Your child consistently sides with your ex. And it seems she is following a script when she is talking about you, using some of the same labels your ex has used to describe you. He will repeat the same words and phrases, as if he is relying on words that are not his own and may have been rehearsed beforehand.

Family ties no longer bind.Your child shows no guilt about her shabby treatment of you. And she not only rejects you, but by extension, your family as well. Formerly beloved aunts, uncles, cousins, and grandparents are now shunned. And your child doesn't want to attend important family events such asweddings, reunions, even funerals.

Influence? What influence?Your child vehemently denies being influenced by your ex. When you note that he is using words and phrases that appear to parrot the other parent, your child dismisses you. In fact, he scoffs at the idea of being coached by anyone.

Since then, everything has changed. She has essentially removed me from all family activities. I do work a lot and cannot be with the family as much as I would like, but she has made it quite clear that she does not want me to be involved in the things she does with our 10 and 13 year old daughters. Now my daughters barely even acknowledge my presence in the room. If I happen to be home when they leave for school, they don't say good bye to me before they leave. When I go to tuck them into bed at night, they recoil from me. When I get home from work and say hello, give them a kiss, and ask them how their day was, I am lucky to get a "fine" from them. When I ask them if they want to do something fun with me, they always say "No"....unless my wife says she is interested. Then they say OK. On top of that, when the kids disrespect me verbally or by their actions in the presence of my wife, she does not correct that behavior. For me, this is the most horrible existence I could have ever imagined.

My wife suffers from Depression and for years I have had to walk on eggshells, turn the other cheek, and hope that "tomorrow will be a better day". I have (and continue to) check my anger at the door....but every once in awhile it boils over, and then I look like the bad guy...so now I think my kids just see me as "the guy who makes mommy sad". And I am sure she helps to reinforce that belief.

I do not know what to do. If I stand firm against her, I am afraid my kids will be more resolved than ever to hate me even more. If I let it continue, I validate their behavior. Her parents are good people, but refuse to get involved....she is an only child (her only brother was killed in an industrial accident 13 years ago....10 days after our first daughter was born). So, in her parents' eyes, she can do no wrong....and they will not stand up to her at all.

Despite all this, I still love my wife, and hope for a day when she will smile every morning and be happy. All I want is for us to be happy, and to have my kids hug me again and say "Hi Daddy, I love you". I would love to take them somewhere for the day by myself for a little one on one (which my wife has never ever allowed me to do in our 13 years of parenthood. I think that thinking comes from her brother's death (they were very close) happening so closely to our first daughter's birth....she is so utterly afraid that something bad will happen to her kids if she is not there to protect them. She will only trust them with her Mom and Dad.But now I am rambling on. I promised myself I would be direct and to the point...but I got lost in all of this. Apologies.

Ultimately, what I want and need is to have my kids like me and want to be with me again. Anybody out there have any advice for me

I find a lot of comfort in reading these comments. Of course, that's because misery loves company...

Sadly, I am a mother of two girls and I have been greatly afflicted by PAS. I have two, grown adult daughters who stayed w/their dad after our divorce; they are now 23 and 25 yrs old. The alienation has been in full force for over 10 yrs now and my girls now have the "independent thinking" that Amy Baker refers to in her books. Meaning, their father no longer has to malign me to them constantly, they've picked up on ways to denigrate me on their own now and see his same short comings in me, so he just sits back now and gloats as their contempt towards me flourishes more and more each day.

Recently, I fell on hard times (I was a victim of a crime and lost everything that I owned) so I had to leave my own residence and return to live (albeit temporarily) w/my ex and daughters in this hostile household. That's a LONG story and the result was not something that either he nor I wanted to have happen. (We short of co-own this house; another long story...) I had nowhere else to go on the spur of the moment, yet we'd been divorced for 4 yrs prior to this new upheaval.

Prior to this tragedy, I had begun to make progress w/my girls once I was independent of their malicious father and out on my own. They had even begun to complain to me about him yet I would just listen and not gossip but that was very hard NOT to do (I sure had to bite my lip!).

Now, these two daughters are almost violent to me. I have tried to explain my temporary set back and dire circumstances to them but they want nothing to do w/me. I was the family bread winner for many years throughout our marriage. When I was recently diagnosed with cancer, my youngest told me that she hopes I die soon and that no one loves me. This was such an awful stab to the heart and I cried for days about this. Having to endure their vicious slings and arrows is much worse then the crime committed against me by a stalker AND my cancer diagnosis, combined. We have a family dog whom I love very much that my daughters try to keep away from me because he often seeks me out, much to their chagrin. When he enters my room, they scream and yell for him and actually chastise the animal once he responds. My daughters tell me that they want me to "rot and burn in hell" as their father passively stands back and says nothing about this horrifically abhorrent behavior.

Today is my eldest daughters birthday. Both she and her boyfriend along w/my other daughter and ex husband are about to go out to dinner to celebrate. I will remain home much like Cinderella was; left to clean out the fireplace. I don't know how my eldest can celebrate her birthday independent of even thinking of me since I was an active participant in that event 25 yrs ago. I told her just to pretend that she was left on the doorstep of her father's home 25 yrs ago by the stork.

I must say I'm a rare parent who does NOT intend to try and heal this rift once I'm out on my own again. Going through cancer and almost dying after two surgeries and not once having my daughters ask how I was feeling when I returned from the hospital has hardened my heart toward them considerably. When the "independent thinking" unfolds, the alienated parent no longer even blames the ex spouse entirely anymore for this behavior - the children have their own set of ideas and opinions that form against us each day so we're left to deflect and defend against them independent of the alienator. I just want to be free of this alienation toxicity and don't care which of those 3 people is targeting me with it.Have any other parents on this site had to turn their backs upon their children as the years have gone by just to maintain their sanity and their health?

In order to live out the rest of my life in peace and avoid future heartaches (like being alienated from eventual grandchildren, etc) I find that with the limited time left in life I don't want to deal with their vile temperaments and growing hostilities. I can choose to be miserable and continue chasing after them for crumbs of acceptance OR I can disengage and focus on being with people who are uplifting, happy and kind.

Sadly, that's not such a hard chose to make in life when a person's reached the end of their rope

adly, I am a mother of two girls and I have been greatly afflicted by PAS. I have two, grown adult daughters who stayed w/their dad after our divorce; they are now 23 and 25 yrs old. The alienation has been in full force for over 10 yrs now and my girls now have the "independent thinking" that Amy Baker refers to in her books. Meaning, their father no longer has to malign me to them constantly, they've picked up on ways to denigrate me on their own now and see his same short comings in me, so he just sits back now and gloats as their contempt towards me flourishes more and more each day.

Recently, I fell on hard times (I was a victim of a crime and lost everything that I owned) so I had to leave my own residence and return to live (albeit temporarily) w/my ex and daughters in this hostile household. That's a LONG story and the end result was not something that either he nor I wanted to have happen. (We short of co-own this house; another long story...) I had nowhere else to go on the spur of the moment, yet we'd been divorced for 4 yrs prior to this new upheaval.

Prior to this tragedy, I had begun to make progress w/my girls once I was independent of their malicious father and out on my own. They had even begun to complain to me about him yet I would just listen and not gossip but that was very hard NOT to do (I sure had to bite my lip!).

Now, these two daughters are almost violent to me. I have tried to explain my temporary set back and dire circumstances to them but they want nothing to do w/me. I was the family bread winner for many years throughout our marriage. When I was recently diagnosed with cancer, my youngest told me that she hopes I die soon and that no one loves me. This was such an awful stab to the heart and I cried for days about this. Having to endure their vicious slings and arrows is much worse then the crime committed against me by a stalker AND my cancer diagnosis, combined.

We have a family dog whom I love very much that my daughters try to keep away from me because he often seeks me out, much to their chagrin. When he enters my room, they scream and yell for him and actually chastise the animal once he responds. My daughters tell me that they want me to "rot and burn in hell" as their father passively stands back and says nothing about this horrifically abhorrent behavior.

Today is my eldest daughters birthday. Both she and her boyfriend along w/my other daughter and ex husband are about to go out to dinner to celebrate. I will remain home much like Cinderella was; left to clean out the fireplace. I don't know how my eldest can celebrate her birthday independent of even thinking of me since I was an active participant in that event 25 yrs. ago. I told her just to pretend that she was left on the doorstep of her father's home 25 yrs. ago by the stork.

I must say I'm a rare parent who does NOT intend to try and heal this rift once I'm out on my own again. Going through cancer and almost dying after two surgeries and not once having my daughters ask how I was feeling when I returned from the hospital has hardened my heart toward them considerably. When the "independent thinking" unfolds, the alienated parent no longer even blames the ex-spouse entirely anymore for this behaviour - the children have their own set of ideas and opinions that form against us each day so we're left to deflect and defend against them independent of the alienator. I just want to be free of this alienation toxicity and don't care which of those 3 people is targeting me with it.

Have any other parents on this site had to turn their backs upon their children as the years have gone by just to maintain their sanity and their health?

In order to live out the rest of my life in peace and avoid future heartaches (like being alienated from eventual grandchildren, etc) I find that with the limited time left in life I don't want to deal with their vile temperaments and growing hostilities. I can choose to be miserable and continue chasing after them for crumbs of acceptance OR I can disengage and focus on being with people who are uplifting, happy and kind

Parental Alienation IS child abuse and emotional abuse ... the following is an outline prepared from the personal experiences of many along with much professional input and attempts to explain in laymans terms various aspects of Parental Alienation.

Parental alienation should not be confused with parental alienation syndrome (PAS) as one is the act of and the other is the result of and in Australia many courts refer to parental alienation as "alignment", parental alienation must have been practiced to have alignment happen.

Parental Alienation is the act of a parent or person coaching/convincing the Children to "break away" from the other parent by way of brainwashing the Children into thinking badly of the targeted Parent often to the point of them refusing to having anything or little to do with that parent, in most cases the Children actually not only believe the words of the Alienator unconditionally at the time but are also coached in such a way as to believe that it is themselves that have made the decission to not love or want to see the other Parent.

Alienators are cunning in their ways and will do almost anything to achieve their goal and this often includes making false allegations of harm to the Children supposedly by the targeted parent that in most cases involves expensive court time and much stress, some targeted parents even give up the fight due to not having the means to meet the expense or choosing not to endure the stress and this is what the alienator wants to happen as it usually results in the targeted parent exiting from the lives of the Children.

The alienator claims to love the Children whilst at the same time their actions are significantly detracting from the Childrens rights, best interests and long term emotional stability, the alienator usually does not care about those things, just to reach their perverted goal at almost any cost, they are acomplished liars and a disgrace to parenthood and there can be many reasons for their actions, mostly perverted and or extremely selfish.

The alienators in most cases know all to well what they are doing to the children and to the targeted parent but once they start they are driven to continue, even into becomming obsessive against the targeted parent ... all at the chidrens cost, alienators will never admit to fault and after some time can even believe themselves that they are not at fault, many even exhibit the signs of various disorders but refuse the sugestions, even professional, indicating such, some back off when they have acieved their goals and others continue for years but in their own minds they are the innocent ones but one thing does not change and that is they are emotionally abusing the children, they are abusing their own children.

The children are "under the spell" of the alienator and especially when young, follow all direction from and adopt all the opinions of the alienator and it is important to remember that ... whatever the children do or say it is not of their own free mind, it is what they are coached/instructed into saying and doing and it is only when they are mature enough that, with or without intervention, they have any chance of working out the truth and discovering their own thoughts and feelings.

Dr. Douglas Darnall in his book Divorce Casualties: Protecting Your Children from Parental Alienation, describes three categories of PA:

MILD: Naïve alienators

Naïve alienators are ignorant of what they are doing and are willing to be educated and change.

MODERATE: Active alienators

When triggered, active alienators lose control of appropriate boundaries. They go ballistic. When they calm down, they don't want to admit that they were out of control.

SEVERE: Obsessed alienators

Obsessed alienators operate from a delusional system where every cell of their body is committed to destroying the other parent's relationship with the child.

In the case of the Obsessed alienator, no treatment exists other than removing the child from their influence.

Here are some scenarios that could be by themselves issues or combined together to make these alienators who they are and why they do what they do.

The alienator is so filled with anger, rage and hatred that they cannot see any further past that and their whole entire world is wrapped around making sure the other person hurts as much as they do. It is like they are blinded by their anger and hatred.

They were raised in a home where one of their parents was an alienator and it is the only thing they know about relationships, that is one person controls everyone and if you do not have control, then you are nothing. So they would not know how to have a relationship any other way nor would they know how to handle it any other way when they loose control over everyone, because to not be in total control means that you are a looser.

The alienator could have such low self-esteem that anyone putting them down or any inference that anything they were involved in was a failure, such as their marriage, would set them off, fighting to defend their honour and reputation. They are so protective of their image, that they will do anything to make sure that they stay looking like the perfect person and destroy everyone else around them to maintain that image.

The alienators own parents put them down constantly and told them they would never amount to much and when their own marriage fails, they are desperate to prove their parents were wrong and will do anything to make it look like it was not their fault.

The alienator's have warped views of themselves from low self- esteem issues. It puts them in such a fragile state of fear that they are no good unless they are seen as all good.

The alienator cannot accept responsibility for their actions and blame them on everyone else because how could they possibly be wrong. Everyone else is wrong.

The alienator is so narcissistic in their beliefs that they are never wrong, to protect that image, they must make sure that they are always on top and that it is everyone's problem or fault.

The alienator was never taught to take responsibility for their own actions and to be humble when they have made a mistake. They were raised that they could do no wrong, just like their own parent/s could do not wrong and thus it is everyone else who is wrong and so Instead they were raised to blame everyone else for their mistakes.

The alienator is so terrified of loosing their children that they have to paint this perfect picture of themselves and make the other person look so bad, to ensure that they do not loose their children and control.

The alienator is so terrified that they are not lovable that they force others to love them.

The alienator is not a real good sharer. In other words, they do not know how to share love and happiness. Maybe because they had to share their parents and never got to understand that sharing is a good thing and feels really good to do.

The alienator often believes that by gaining total control of the children prior to any property settlement that they will benefit financially from same and that they will recieve maximum ongoing financial support from agencies like child support and social security should they have significant custody of the children.

It is usually the alienator that ends the relationship with the other parent and looks to justify their decission to friends and family by making out the other parent was at fault and not worthy of any consideration in the process, they cannot accept responsability for their own actions.

The alienator may have a disorder such as borderline personality disorder.

Eight Behaviors of a Child Being Manipulated;

Expletives and Bad-mouthing: The child denigrates the alienated parent with foul language and severe oppositional behaviour.

Excuses without Foundation: The child offers weak, absurd or frivolous reasons for his or her anger.

Consistently Negative: The child is sure of him or herself, never swaying from a negative connotation. He/she doesn't demonstrate confused emotions (i.e. love and hate) for the alienated parent, only the negative hate.

Self-righteous: The child exhorts that he or she alone came up with ideas of denigration. The "independent-thinker" phenomenon is where the child asserts that no one told him to do this.

Protective: supports and feels a need to protect the alienating parent.

Lack of Empathy: the child does not demonstrate guilt over cruelty towards the alienated parent.

Lying & embellishing: the child uses borrowed scenarios or vividly describes situations that he or she could not have experienced.

Anger: Animosity is spread to the friends and/or extended family of the alienated parent.

The alienators "tools of trade".

Many alienators will not come out and degrade the targeted openly (many do), some use more subtle methods and when you think you have heard it all more come to light, although some use only a few others use many, here are some;

Sympathy ... alienators often use sympathy to gain the loyalty of the children, this can be as simple as "he/she left us with no money and does not care about us", sympathy from friends and family is important also as the alienator sees this as loyalty, support and justification for their actions ... "I cry and miss you terribly when you stay over at his/her place", not hard to guess what the children are left with on this one, they do not want to see the alienator hurt, anyone for that matter but the targeted do not usually say things like this so the children do not think the alienator does miss them or get hurt when they are not with the targeted.

Emotional support ... by enlisting the childrens emotional support the children become loyal at the cost of the other parent, here the alienator sets out to have the children feel sorry for the alienator and to have negative attitudes towards the targeted, the children are made to feel they have to support the alienator and in many cases are also made to feel that if they continue to love the targeted that the alienator will be let down.

False allegations of abuse ... one of the favourites, this can be and mostly is sexual abuse against the children, this is a Biggy and hits hard to the innocent targeted parent and often results in that parent not seeing the children for some time or only under supervision after some time and then court proceedings all of which are expensive and emotionally draining, here the alienator is hoping the targeted will just give up and walk away or to give in to unreasonable demands, usually financial.

Control ... the alienator has to feel in control and will do almost anything to get it and an example here is "if you do that then this may happen (bad)", leaving the children to make the decission that the alienator wanted all along.

The power of Suggestive comments ... "you make sure that he/she looks after you when you are there, make sure that you get enough food and tell me if you don't", when a child hears this type of comment they immediately become suspicious and concerned with the targeted parent, and will often report negatively about their stay to the alienator knowing the alienator is expecting it.

Trying to buy love ... the alienator will most likely have the children prepared that should you give them something that they don't have at the alienators place their comment will be "you cannot buy our love with gifts", the real side of this is the children think they do not love you and that you cannot secure their love, the alienator will have gone to great lengths on this one so that whatever you do they may well refuse to love you.

Name changing ... the alienator in many case's tries to change the childrens surnames and has the children believe that their new name is a better name and possibly that your surname has a bad reputation and that is why the change, the alienator will have justified the attempt to change their name to the children in some way.

"Does he/she treat and speak to you properly" ... a simple thing like you raising your voice will be and indication to the children that you don't, by the time the alienator has finished with this one you will have shouted at them and the alienator will have said things like "if he/she shouted at you then he/she does not respect or love you", it is not the alienator making the decission about you, the children based on what the alienator has explained will make the decission that you do not respect or love them.   This is a favourite method used by an alienator, just supply a well crafted and pointed basis for a decission and let them make it to the negative when it suits the alienator. The children will most likely be lead to feel that you are not deserving of their love and affection because you treat them badly, anything that you may do or say apart from being perfect may be used against you in this way.

Your family and friends ... in most cases the alienator will attempt to discredit them also ... "his/her brother, your uncle, is a fat alcoholic drug using nobody" ... now if this is true there may be some fair basis but by now it is true in the children's minds, especially if the uncle is fat, and whilst the alienator has not targeted you directly they have discredited you, by association. The alienator uses some fact to strengthen a lie and all the children see is the fact that the uncle is fat so the rest must be true. Discredit enough of your friends and family and you are discredited in the eyes of the children.

Home is where the heart is ... and rightfully so but the alienator takes every opportunity to drive this home and that their heart really belongs at the alienators place ... "are you happier here or over there" ... the children do not want to disappoint so they say here and if gone over enough it becomes reality, it is a lot easier for them that way and the end result is that they do not feel at home at the the other parents place hence no or little love or sense of belonging at the home of the targeted, end result is that they do not want to be there.

"If you loved us you would just want us to be happy" ... and by now guess where they think (coached) they are the happiest ... "if you loved us you would just want us to be happy and you would not care what the judge said, you would let us go" ... this is a very difficult one as by the time they have got up the courage to say it (coached) then they really think it and then you become the baddy by not letting them go. The alienator knows you won't so again you loose.

Holidays ... do not tell the children where you plan to take them on holidays, if you do they will most likely tell the alienator giving the alienator an opportunity to discredit the event by pointing out the dangers etc ... camping, "be carefull of all the snakes and spiders" ... in the end the children are not keen to go and the excitement of it all is gone, you have made the bookings and they do not want to go but you go and they are angry with you even after they have settled down and ultimately enjoy the holiday ... "it is dangerous to take children camping in the bush" leaves the children thinking you are willing to put them in danger, not a good parent.

This site was prepared and is run by private individuals who have felt the pain ... there is no commercial affiliation of any type whatsoever.

The end of a romantic relationship is always difficult for parents. It can be just as difficult, if not worse, for their children. How children deal with the end of their parents' relationship has to do with two things: the age and maturity of the children, and how their parents manage the breakdown of their relationship.

Children don't see things in terms of "custody" or "parental responsibilities" when their parents' relationship ends. All they know is that something has gone wrong. Mom and dad are yelling at each other a lot, and then, one day, mom or dad isn't there anymore. Young children won't understand these adult problems. Children who are in primary school will have a better idea, since they'll have friends whose parents have separated. Pre-teens and teens may seem to have a much more grown-up grasp of things as they'll have lost relationships of their own, and may be able to appreciate the idea that their parents' relationship has ended. How children cope with their parents' separation changes as they grow older and more mature.

Things are a lot different for parents. A significant relationship has ended, and in the midst of all of the emotions that go along with that — grief, anger, jealousy, love and loss — they might find themselves also having to deal with some extremely difficult legal issues. It's even worse where the parents wind up fighting about things in court.

Litigation can have a very profound impact on people. At its core, litigation is an adversarial process: each parent is fighting the other in order to "win," and where there's a winner there's always a loser. This sort of approach to a dispute often polarizes parents and encourages them to take extreme positions. What makes this so much worse is that the parents are both fighting about something they cherish dearly, their children, and they are both fighting against someone whom they used to deeply love.

In circumstances like these, it can be easy to forget how important it is that the children maintain a positive, loving relationship with the other parent. It can also be easy to overlook the importance of managing the children's exposure to and perception of their parents' conflict. One parent's view of the other becomes clouded by hatred, malice and spite, and nothing the other parent can do is ever right. This attitude is almost impossible to shield from the children. Whether intentionally or unintentionally, the children are inevitably exposed to these negative views which, without interference, can come to colour the children's own views of the other parent.

Children's experiences of separation

It is important to remember that while one parent's thoughtless comments about the other parent can have an impact on how a child sees the other parent, so too will the child's own experience of the separation. This can include:

blaming the parent who left for breaking up the family,

seeing a parent as injured by the actions of the other parent,

sympathizing with an emotionally upset parent, and

missing and feeling sad for the parent that they see less often.

These feelings may have nothing at all to do with any blameworthy conduct on the part of either parent, but they can cause a child to feel closer to one parent than the other. Further, there a number of normal reasons why a child might feel closer to one parent even in families that haven't separated, such as:

similarities in the temperament of the child and one of the parents,the parent's gender,interests the child shares with a parent, and how the parent handles discipline.

There are, of course, ways that parents can behave, intentionally and unintentionally, that will encourage a child to drift towards one parent and away from the other that are blameworthy. Remember, however, that there are normal reasons why a child's experience of divorce may align with one parent over the other that have nothing to do with a parent's conduct.

Resisting visits with a parent

When a child begins to drift apart from a parent, the first sign that this might become a serious problem often occurs when the child begins to express a reluctance to spend time with the other parent. It is important to distinguish a simple reluctance from a more serious problem like estrangement or alienation. It is also important to distinguish between a reluctance that stems from a child and a reluctance that is fostered by a parent. In a sense, this is the key difference between estrangement and alienation.

Normal reasons why a child might resist parenting time or contact include age-appropriate separation anxieties,

inability to cope with the transition between homes, especially where there is a lot of conflict between the parents,

not wanting to leave an upset parent at home, and

not liking the other parent's parenting style.

Of course, any resistance to separation is difficult for both parents. For the parent sending the child on the visit, it can be heart wrenching to force the child out the door. For the parent receiving the child, it can be devastating to hear — from the other parent or the child — that the parenting time or contact is unwelcome, and to experience the rejection that this entails.

These "normal" reasons why a child would be reluctant to see a parent can be aggravated by the unintentional conduct of each parent. Separated parents have a positive duty to nurture their child's relationship with the other parent. In the context of parenting time and contact, this means encouraging the child to look forward to seeing the other parent. In general, this means actively fostering the child's relationship with the other parent and refraining from making negative remarks about the other parent.

In high-conflict situations, even parents who understand this basic duty can unconsciously telegraph their feelings about the other parent to the child. Children are not stupid; they know something's not right. Even young children will pick up on non-verbal clues to a parent's feelings.

This sort of unintentional communication of emotion includes:

making faces, grimacing, groaning, cringing or shuddering when the other parent is mentioned,

arguing with the other parent when the children can see or hear the dispute,

making negative comments about the other parent when the children are within earshot,

using an emotionless or negative tone of voice when speaking to the children about the other parent, and

reacting in a flat or negative manner when the children discuss the other parent or their activities with that parent.

Even though in these examples nothing is actually being said to the children to discourage their relationship with the other parent, they will pick up on the implications these behaviours suggest: there is something bad about one parent which is hurting the other parent. This sort of behaviour will inevitably encourage and reinforce any resistance the child might have to seeing the other parent.

When a child begins to express a reluctance to visit the other parent, both parents must act to stop the problem from getting worse.

For the parent who has the child most often, this means that you must:

work harder at encouraging the child to look forward to the visits,

make sure that you are not a part of the problem by unconsciously telegraphing your problems with the other parent,

make an effort to remind the child about the other parent's positive traits,

consider getting the child in to see a counsellor about the separation, and

seriously consider taking a parenting after separation course.

For the parent whom the child is resisting seeing, this means that you must:

work harder at making the child feel welcomed and listened to in your home,

re-examine your approach to parenting issues, particularly if you were the disciplinarian during your relationship with the other parent,

make sure that you are not insulting or mocking the other parent when the child is within earshot, and

seriously consider taking a parenting after separation course.

None of these solutions may be effective if the child's opinion and emotions are too entrenched, if the parents are simply too angry with one another to cooperate effectively, or if one of the parents is actively working to undermine the other parent's relationship with the child.

When things go too far, or when a problem is left unchecked, a child's simple preference for one parent can develop to an extreme point, where the child is estranged or alienated from the other parent.

Knowing when there's a problem

An otherwise "normal" resistance to parenting time or contact can cross the line when the child's opinion of the parent and his or her emotional attachment to that parent begins to change. Temper tantrums about a visit, and expressions of rage and hate should send a loud and clear signal that both parents have to work a lot harder to help the child through his or her experience of the separation.

Mild expressions of a change in the child's attachment to a parent include:

Expressing ambivalence about visiting the parent (not caring one way or the other about seeing the parent).

Grumbling about having to go to see the other parent.

Stating a preference for an activity (playing a game, seeing friends and so forth) over seeing the other parent.

More serious expressions of a change in the child's attachment to a parent include:

Expressing a preference for one parent over the other, and a general ambivalence about the other parent.

Expressing a preference for one home over the other.

Expressing a worry about missing the parent the child is leaving.

Being upset that an activity (playing a game, an outing, seeing friends and so forth) will be interrupted by the visit.

Stating that visits with other parent are boring.

Being reluctant to speak to the other parent on the telephone.

Still more serious expressions of a change include

Stating that he or she "doesn't like" the other parent.

Occasionally putting the other parent down.

Expressions of concern for the well-being of the parent the child is leaving for the visit (older children).

Crying before the visit (younger children).

Complaining that "it's not fair" to have to visit (older children).

Don’t believe what they say: that Parental Alienation cannot happen to older children, that it’s just an oxymoron.

Parental Alienation is the act of one parent deliberately undermining the relationship between the children and the other parent to the point of creating a hostile relationship and thus alienation of the children from the other parent. Another way to look at this is alienation of affection, which is one of the basic human needs discussed at length by Maslow in his Hierarchy of Needs. It is a

serious form of psychological abuse, and it is very dangerous because it occurs internally and, thus, is harder to treat. Unlike physical abuse where the scars and wounds are on the outside, Parental Alienation Syndrome (PAS) is so deep inside that unlocking the key to it takes years of treatment and unconditional love.

Though PAS is primarily seen in high-conflict divorces, it also occurs in intact families. And though it usually begins in early childhood, this is not always the case, and does not mean that older children and even adults cannot be alienated from their other parent. In fact, PAS is often described as a cult form of control over others. In this respect, we can say that the perpetrator or

alienator brainwashes and programs the innocent victims to hate their other parent/family members. In much the way as the leaders of cults, like Jonestown, these perpetrators are able to take a person and convert him or her into the alienator's way of thinking and to renounce all ties with the victim's families and friends. If a cult leader can do this to total strangers who have no familial ties to them, then it is safe to say that it would be that much easier for a parent to do this to his or her children, no matter what age they are.

Parents and family have a much stronger bind or hold upon children. In fact, a child, no matter what age, would be more likely to listen to and believe his or her parent than a total stranger. Therefore, any judge, counselor, agency or attorney claiming that an older child could not be alienated from his or her other parent, is actually stating that cults, like the Branch Davidians, could not possibly happen. In these non-believers' minds, only children can be brainwashed and programmed. This defies logic, as it is a proven fact that cults do brainwash people and program them, and most of these cult followers are adults. In other words, if a total stranger can turn a person against his or her family, then a parent can do it even more easily, no matter the age of the child.

Furthermore, as Amy J. L. Baker points out in her book, Adult Children of Parental Alienation Syndrome – Breaking the Ties that Bind, adolescents are just as vulnerable to the tactics used to impede a relationship with the other parent. These young adults are at a point in their lives where they are allowed more responsibility to make their own decisions, and one of those is custody and visitation. Baker feels that alienators are probably quite aware of this and utilize this idea as they intensify their tactics to distance the children from the other parent. In addition to this issue, young adults are struggling for their independence from their parents and if one parent, the alienator, offers them more freedom and thus are more liberal with them, the children will be swayed easily to side with this parent. Alienators know this very well, and actually use this same technique when bribing their children monetarily with gifts and toys. (Baker, p. 182-183) Alienators are good exploiters of weaknesses in people. They will go after the weakest link to break the chain and command control of the other links in the chain. What better way to do this than with bribery and offerings.

Case in point: two children who are raised since birth to hate their father's side of his family. The children are repeatedly told that relatives from their father's side of the family are no good and crazy and that the children are never to spend time alone with them. Their mother even tries to convince their father that his side of the family is not good and actually rarely lets the kids visit their paternal grandparents, niece, or nephew. Fast-forward 15 years, to a failed marriage. Though the children have spent very positive and rewarding times with their father and his family especially during the holiday seasons, in the back of their minds, they have been programmed to not trust them. So when the father initiates a divorce, instantly the mother begins to denigrate and berate the father. The children, though 14 and 16, are easily turned against their father and refuse to spend time with him, and when they do, they are disrespectful and rude. Despite the judge's orders, these two teenagers are too enmeshed with their mother's hatred, anger, and faulty beliefs that their relationship with their father is near non-existent. Despite 15 years of positive good memories that they could draw upon, the years of programming and brainwashing have taken their toll. PAS does not differentiate age. PAS does not prejudice only the very young. PAS is real and can affect anyone of any age and gender. It is ageless, genderless and most of all, the most painful form of psychological abuse a guardian can inflict on another human being. Until the judges, counsellors, agencies and attorneys accept the fact that PAS has no preferences and can occur to anyone at any time in his or her life, this form of Domestic Violence will continue to grow and destroy families

There is an old African proverb that states "when two elephants fight it is the grass under their feet that suffers". Similarly, when parents fight over custody and access of their children after a separation it is the children that suffer. In many cases the parents are not even aware of the effect that their custody battle is having on their children and they do not intend to hurt their children. Nevertheless, research shows that children who have lived through a high conflict divorce have a greater tendency to develop mental health issues, addiction issues, are less likely to obtain a post-secondary education and have a whole host of other social problems that develop later on in their lives as a result of their negative experience.

In some of the more extreme high conflict custody cases, a dynamic develops whereby one of the parents sets out to sever the children's ties to the other parent. The American psychiatrist who first coined the phrase "parental alienation" described it as, "a disorder that arises primarily in the context of child custody disputes. Its primary manifestation is the child's campaign of denigration against a parent, a campaign that has no justification. It results from the combination of a programming parent's indoctrinations and the child's own contributions to the vilification of the target parent." Some of the symptoms of Parental Alienation Syndrome which will be added as a diagnosis under the DSM in 2010, are as follows

The alienated child:

- Sees one parent as all good and other parent as all bad;

- Appears to really hate "bad parent" and hates their family

· When they talk about alienated parent appear to be putting on a show – affect does not match their words

Rewrites family history sometimes to involve stories of sexual and physical abuse by other parent

· Involves child in litigation by reading court documents to him/her and or using child as messenger

· Puts child in position where he/she is forced to choose between their parents

As with most things in life, there is a wide spectrum of severity and the blame usually does not fall on one person's shoulders only. The "alienated parent" often contributes to the problem by making the child feel guilty, rejecting the child, acting aggressively towards the child or to the other parent or by simply giving up hope and abandoning the child. Also, some children are estranged from a parent prior to the separation and it only gets worse after wards. The alienating parents often act the way they do because they feel that they have been abandoned by the other parent and are very hurt by the separation. They themselves may have been abandoned or abused as children.

Richard Gardner and some of his followers are of the view that the only cure to this problem is to take the child out of the custody of the alienating parent, subject the child to intense counseling to de-brainwash the child and then place the child in the alienated parent's custody.

Not surprisingly, there are many family court judges who do not accept that this is the only solution to the problem. Instead, they try to affect a change in the dynamic by making access orders enforceable by the police, making a parent who is withholding access pay a fine or even ordering that the alienating parent go to jail if they breach the access order again.

In the US there are some residential programs available for families with this problem. In Canada, there are therapists who specialize in assisting families with this problem, but there are no residential programs that I am aware of.

In my view the essential thing is to prevent the alienation from happening in the first place. This can be done by identifying the early symptoms and ensuring that there is an access plan in place very shortly after the separation that is strongly enforced by the court. It is also essential that all parties involved get counseling to identify the issues that are at the root of the problem and bring them to the surface and that professionals involved in helping parents who are separating and divorcing are trained to recognize the early symptoms.

There have been recent amendments made to the Children's Law Reform Act to reinforce the idea that maximum contact with both parents is generally in the best interests of children and that parents have an obligation not only to allow access, but to facilitate that access.

If you are fearful that this dynamic may be occurring in your family, please don't wait for things to get better. Parental alienation is like cancer- if left untreated it will grow and kill your relationship with your child. Children in families where there is this dynamic are "victims" of abuse and end up exhibiting the same symptoms as children who are physically and sexually abused by their family members. You have a responsibility to protect your children from this abuse, as do all the professionals who are involved in your case.

Parental alienation syndrome (PAS) and parental alienation (PA) are often invoked in legal and legislative contexts addressing the rights of fathers and mothers in custody or visitation litigation. Indeed, alienation claims have become ubiquitous in custody cases where domestic violence or child abuse is alleged, as grounds to reject mothers' requests to limit paternal access to their children. This paper provides a historical and research overview of PAS and PA, identifies strategic issues for advocates working with abused women and children,* and offers guidelines to improve courts' treatment of these issues. While PAS and PA have much in common both as theories and with respect to how they are used in court, they have distinct scientific and research bases and critiques. This paper, therefore, addresses them separately.

Parental Alienation Syndrome

Historical Background

The notion of children's hostility to one parent in the context of divorce was first characterized as a pathology by divorce researchers Wallerstein and Kelly. They theorized that a child's rejection of a noncustodial parent and strong resistance or refusal to visit that parent was sometimes a "pathological" alignment between an angry custodial parent and an older child or adolescent and that this alliance was fueled by the dynamics of marital separation, including a child's reaction to it (Wallerstein & Kelly, 1976, 1980). Although significant, Wallerstein and Kelly's construct did not become a staple of custody evaluations or judicial determinations. Moreover, their early work does not use the phrase "parental alienation," but focuses instead on children's "alignment" with one parent against the other.

Beginning in the early 1980's, attention to a purported "parental alienation syndrome" exploded as the result of the dedicated efforts of Richard Gardner, a psychiatrist loosely affiliated with Columbia Medical School1 who ran a clinical practice that focused on counselling divorcing parents.

Based solely on his interpretation of data gathered from his clinical practice, Gardner posited that child sexual abuse allegations were rampant in custody litigation, and that 90% of children in custody litigation suffered from a disorder, which he called "Parental Alienation Syndrome (PAS)." He described PAS as a "syndrome" whereby vengeful mothers employed child abuse allegations as a powerful weapon to punish ex-husbands and ensure custody to themselves (Gardner, 1992a; 1992b). He further theorized that such mothers enlisted the children in their "campaign of denigration" and "vilification" of the father, that they often "brainwashed" or "programmed" the children into believing untrue claims of abuse by the father, and that the children then fabricated and contributed their own stories (Gardner, 1992b, p. 162, 193; 2002, pp. 94-95). He claimed – based solely on his own interpretation of his own clinical experience – that the majority of child sexual abuse claims in custody litigation are false (Gardner, 1991), although he suggested that some mothers' vendettas were the product of pathology rather than intentional malice (Gardner,

1987, 1992b). In short, Gardner claimed that when children reject their father and they or their mother makes abuse allegations, this behavior is most likely the product of PAS rather than actual experiences of abuse. PAS theory is thus premised on the assumption that child abuse claimants' believability and trustworthiness is highly suspect.2

While acknowledging that if there was actually abuse which explained a child's hostility there could be no PAS (Gardner, 1992a), Gardner's "diagnostic criteria" focused on various personality characteristics of the accuser, accused, and the child, rather than expert assessments of abuse itself or the other reasons that might explain a child's hostility to a parent (Gardner, 1992b; see also Hoult, 2006). Rather, Gardner's PAS theory presumes that a child's hostility to a father is pathological, which, in turn, encourages courts to suspect that mothers who make such allegations are doing so only to undermine the child's relationship with the father. Indeed, in differentiating between "fabricated" and "bona fide" abuse, Gardner uses "the Presence of the Parental Alienation Syndrome" as itself an "extremely valuable differentiating [criterion]" (Gardner, 1987, p. 109). By PAS, as previously discussed, he means a child's "campaign of denigration" of the father and the mother's supposed "programming" of the child/ren (Gardner, 2002, pp. 95-97). In short, Gardner's PAS theory essentially presumes PAS's existence from the mere presence of a child's hostility toward and/or fear of their father based on alleged abuse. This is unfortunately precisely how it has been applied in many courts.

It should be further noted that the "Sexual Abuse Legitimacy Scale," which Gardner invented as a means of quantifying the likelihood that sexual abuse claims were valid, was so excoriated by scientific experts as "garbage" that he withdrew the scale; however, many of the factors it contained continue to be part of his qualitative discussions of how to determine whether child sexual abuse allegations are legitimate (Bruch, 2001; Faller, 1998).

Gardner's Remedies for PAS

Gardner's "remedy" for purportedly severe PAS is extreme - including complete denial of maternal-child contact and "de-programming" the child through a concerted brainwashing effort to change the child's beliefs that they have been abused (Bruch, 2001; Gardner, 1992a; see also www.rachelfoundation.org). After being subjected to these procedures and ordered by the court to live with the father they said abused them, some children became suicidal and some killed themselves (Bruch, 2001; Hoult, 2006). In other cases, courts have ordered children into jail and juvenile homes as part of Gardner's recommended "threat therapy" which is the stock in trade of strict alienation psychologists (Hoult, 2006; Johnston & Kelly, 2004a). In one such case, a judge ordered a frail nine-year-old boy seized by three police officers and placed in a juvenile detention facility when he refused to get into his father's car for a scheduled visitation. The son of the father's girlfriend had sexually abused the boy, and he had also witnessed the father's violence against his mother. After three days of abuse by the other boys in the detention facility, the boy agreed to cooperate with the court order. The judge concluded that his "treatment" for parental alienation had worked (E. Stark, personal communication, May 2007).

As critiques of PAS have pointed out, PAS is a teflon defense to an accusation of abuse, because all evidence brought to bear to support the abuse claims is simply reframed as further evidence of the "syndrome" (Bruch, 2001). That is, all efforts to gather corroboration of the allegations are simply treated as further evidence of her pathological need to "alienate" the child from the father (Gardner, 1987, 1992a). If the protective parent points to a therapist's opinion that the child has been abused, the therapist is accused of a "folie a trois" (a clinical term from the French for "folly of three") which suggests that all three parties are in a dysfunctional "dance" together (Bruch, 2001). A child's or a protective parent's repetition of claims of abuse is routinely characterized as further evidence of extreme alienation, and punished by court orders prohibiting continued reporting of abuse.

Gardner's pro-pedophilic and misogynistic beliefs

Gardner's underlying beliefs regarding human sexuality, including adult-child sexual interaction, are so extreme and unfounded that it is hard to believe that courts would have adopted his theory had they known. First, he asserted that the reason women lie about child sexual abuse in custody litigation is because "hell hath no fury like a woman scorned" (Gardner, 1992b, pp. 218-19), and/or because they are "gratifie[d] vicariously" (Gardner, 1991, p. 25; 1992a, p. 126) by imagining their child having sex with the father. There is of course no empirical basis or support for these offensive assertions.

Second, Gardner's views of sexuality were disturbing. He claimed that all human sexual paraphilias, including pedophilia, sadism, rape, necrophilia, zoophilia (sex with animals), coprophilia (sex with feces), and other deviant behaviors "serve the purposes of species survival" by "enhanc[ing] the general level of sexual excitation in society" (Gardner, 1992b, p. 20; see also Hoult, 2006; Dallam, 1998.)

Further, Gardner claimed that women's physiology and conditioning makes them potentially masochistic rape victims who may "gain pleasure from being beaten, bound, and otherwise made to suffer," as "the price they are willing to pay for gaining the gratification of receiving the sperm" (Gardner, 1992b, p. 26).

Regarding pedophilia, Gardner argued expressly that adult-child sex need not be intrinsically harmful to children, and that it is beneficial to the species, insofar as it increases a child's sexualization and increases the likelihood that his or her genes will be transmitted at an early age (Gardner, 1992b). Gardner claimed, "sexual activities between an adult and a child are an ancient tradition" and phenomenon which "has been present in just about every society studied, both past and present" (Gardner, 1992b, pp. 47-48). He viewed Western society as "excessively punitive" in its treatment of pedophilia as a "sickness and a crime" (Gardner, 1991, p. 115), and attributed this "overreaction" to the influence of the Jews (Gardner, 1992b, pp. 47, 49). Gardner opposed mandated reporting of child sexual abuse and specifically described a case in which he successfully persuaded a mother not to report a bus driver who had molested her daughter, because it would "interfere with the natural desensitization process, would be likely to enhance guilt, and would have other untoward psychological effects" (Gardner, 1992b, pp. 611-12; see also Dallam, 1998). Gardner's perspective on adult-child sexual interaction can be summed up in his reference to Shakespeare's famous quote: "'There is nothing either good or bad, but thinking makes it so'" (Gardner, 1991, p. 115).

Despite his assertions that pedophilia is widespread and harmless, he asserted in a filmed interview that a child who tells his mother he has been sexually molested by his or her father should be told "I don't believe you. I'm going to beat you for saying it. Don't you ever talk that way again about your father" (Waller, 2001).3 This response – and his beliefs described above – suggest that the animating intention behind the PAS theory's denial of the validity of child sexual abuse reports is not a genuine belief that child sexual abuse is often falsely reported, but rather a belief that such reports should be suppressed.

While Gardner and PAS have had many adherents, particularly among forensic evaluators and litigants, there is actually no empirical research validating the existence of PAS. And there is extensive empirical proof that the assumptions underlying the theory are false.

Sole empirical study of PAS does not validate the concept. Only one study has been published that purports to empirically verify the existence of PAS. Consistent with scientific standards, this study sought to assess the "inter-rater reliability" of PAS – i.e., the extent to which different observers can consistently identify PAS (Rueda, 2004). The study built directly on Gardner's criteria, taking for granted that those criteria reflect PAS. It then measured the degree to which a small sample of therapists agreed on whether five case scenarios presented to them reflect those PAS criteria or not (Rueda, 2004). The findings were that there was a reasonable degree of agreement about whether these cases indicated PAS. However, the findings do not prove its existence – rather, they prove that a small number of mental health professionals agreed on applying the label PAS to cases of estranged ("alienated") children. Many therapists surveyed, however, had refused to fill out the questionnaire and some expressly stated they didn't believe PAS existed. This study thus simply presumed rather than proved the key question: is the concept of PAS actually a disorder caused by a malevolent aligned parent's efforts, or is it simply a reframing of a child's estrangement flowing from abuse, other problematic conduct by the alienated parent, or other normative reasons? The author himself admits that the findings did not "differentiate PAS from parental alienation" (Rueda, 2004, p. 400). Since "parental alienation" is merely a label that does not in itself explain the reason for the child's alienation, this admission essentially negates the study as a validator of PAS. PAS' empirical bases are false or unsupported. The claims upon which Gardner based his PAS theory are thoroughly contradicted by the empirical research. First, Gardner (1991, 1992b) claimed that child sexual abuse allegations are widespread in custody cases and that the vast majority of such allegations are false. These claims have no empirical basis, other than Gardner's interpretation of his own clinical practice. In contradiction, the largest study of child sexual abuse allegations in custody litigation ever conducted found that child sexual abuse allegations were extremely rare (less than 2% of cases) and of those, approximately 50% of the claims were deemed valid, even when assessed by normally conservative court and agency evaluators (Thoennes & Tjaden, 1990). Other studies have found such allegations to be validated approximately 70% of the time (Faller, 1998).

Moreover, leading researchers have found that the dominant problem in child sexual abuse evaluation is not false allegations, but rather, the "high rates of unsubstantiated maltreatment" in "circumstances that indicat[e] that abuse or neglect may have occurred" (Trocme & Bala, 2005, pp. 1342-44).

Indeed, empirical research has found that the PAS theory is built upon an assumption which is the opposite of the truth: Where PAS presumes that protective mothers are vengeful and pathologically "program" their children, it is not women and children – but noncustodial fathers – who are most likely to fabricate child maltreatment claims. In the largest study of its kind, leading researchers analyzed the 1998 Canadian Incidence Study of Reported Child Abuse and Neglect. They found that only 12% of child abuse or neglect allegations made in the context of litigation over child access were intentionally false (Trocme & Bala, 2005). Notably, they found that the primary source (43%) of these intentionally false reports was noncustodial parents (typically fathers); relatives, neighbors, or acquaintances accounted for another 19% of false reports. Only 14% of knowingly false claims were made by custodial parents (typically mothers), and only two cases (out of 308) fit the alienation paradigm of an intentionally false abuse allegations against a noncustodial father (Trocme & Bala, 2005).

PAS has been rejected as invalid by scientific and professional authorities. The dominant consensus in the scientific community is that there is no scientific evidence of a clinical "syndrome" concerning "parental alienation." Leading researchers, including some who treat "alienation" itself as a real problem, concur, "The scientific status of PAS is, to be blunt, nil" (Emery, Otto, & O'Donohue, 2005, p. 10; see also Gould, 2006; Johnston & Kelly, 2004b; Myers, Berliner, Briere, Hendrix, Jenny, and Reid, 2002; Smith and Coukos, 1997; Wood, 1994). The Presidential Task Force of the American Psychological Association on Violence in the Family stated as early as 1996 that "[a]lthough there are no data to support the phenomenon called parental alienation syndrome, in which mothers are blamed for interfering with their children's attachment to their fathers, the term is still used by some evaluators and Courts to discount children's fears in hostile and psychologically abusive situations" (p. 40). Dr. Paul Fink, past President of the American Psychiatric Association, describes PAS as "junk science" (Talan, 2003, line 9). Nonetheless, defences of PAS against critiques have led even some respected social scientists to mis-cite and distort the research.

Thus, PAS has been rejected multiple times by the American Psychiatric Association as lacking in scientific basis and therefore not worthy of inclusion in the Diagnostic and Statistical Manual of Mental Disorders. The most recent all-out campaign by PAS proponents for inclusion of (the re-named) "Parental Alienation Disorder" (PAD) was flatly rejected by the DSM-V committee in 2012 (Crary, 2012).

Echoing the scientific consensus, a leading judicial body, the National Council of Juvenile and Family Court Judges (NCJFCJ), has published guidelines for custody courts stating:

[t]he discredited "diagnosis" of "PAS" (or allegation of "parental alienation"), quite apart from its scientific invalidity, inappropriately asks the court to assume that the children's behaviors and attitudes toward the parent who claims to be "alienated" have no grounding in reality. It also diverts attention away from the behaviors of the abusive parent, who may have directly influenced the children's responses by acting in violent, disrespectful, intimidating, humiliating and/or discrediting ways toward the children themselves, or the children's other parent

In contrast to PAS theory that views the indoctrinating parent as the principal player in the child's alienation, this study [their own] found that children's rejection of a parent had multiple determinants . . . [another study of theirs also] supported a multi-dimensional explanation of children's rejection of a parent, with both parents as well as vulnerabilities within the child contributing to the problem. Alienating behavior by an emotionally needy aligned parent (mother or father), with whom the child was in role-reversal, were strong predictors of the child's rejection of the other parent. Just as important as contributors were critical incidents of child abuse and/or lack of warm, involved parenting by the rejected parent (pp. 80-81).

Johnston also differentiates her approach from Gardner's by rejecting his draconian "remedies," including custody switching to the "hated" parent. Characterizing Gardner's prescriptions as "a license for tyranny," Johnston and Kelly (2004b, p. 85) call instead for individualized assessments of both the children and the parents' parenting, maintaining focus on the children's needs rather than the parents' rights. In theory, the goal is a more realistic and healthy relationship with both parents, rather than reconciliation with the hated parent as the only desirable goal (Johnston, 2005). Unfortunately, the common practice in court is far less nuanced and individualized (see below).

The notion that some children are alienated from a parent is both a less scientific and more factual assertion. It is thus easier to raise "alienation" in court without triggering a battle over the admissibility of scientific evidence (Gardner, 2002). However, debate continues to rage in research and advocacy circles over the extent to which parental alienation is something that can be measured, is caused by a parent, and/or has truly harmful effects, or whether it is simply a new less objectionable name for the invalidated PAS. To the extent that PA is widely used almost identically to PAS in court, it may not matter in practice what the theoretical differences are.

Critique of PA - Lack of Evidence Base

Questioning the scientific basis of parental alienation and PAS is challenging because these theories are described and referenced in a substantial social science literature (Turkat, 2002). Many of these materials make assertions about PAS and PA without any citation to scientific literature – yet their "publication" on the Internet and their association with apparently credentialed authors and/or supporters, give them an aura of credibility. Some articles do cite research selectively, but contain numerous unsupported assertions as well, about PAS, PA, and how they operate.

Custody evaluators and psychologists frequently insist as an anecdotal matter that alienation is present and is a terrible thing. However, the only existing empirical basis for this assumption of alienation's harmfulness at this time is limited to "clinical observation" (Johnston & Kelly, 2004b; see also Ackerman & Dolezal, 2006). Of course clinical observations are subjective, and do not constitute empirical evidence. Moreover, these statements do not indicate whether the relationship breaches between children and parents observed by these clinicians are a healthy or developmental response to their relationship with that parent, or if the "alienation" is wrongfully instigated by a favored ("aligned") parent (Johnston & Kelly, 2004b). Indeed, even if the clinical observers attempted to make the distinction, there would be no objective way of discerning whether their judgment was correct (short of a comprehensive assessment of the child-parent relationship, including any abusive, neglectful or cold, indifferent or hostile parenting by the disliked parent.

In fact, what the empirical evidence Johnston et al. (2005) have amassed indicates both that (i) actual “alienation” of a child is quite rare despite many parents’ derogatory conduct or statements about the other parent and (ii) when children are estranged from a parent there are always multiple reasons, some of which are that parent’s own conduct. Their widely published research has found that, despite the alienating behaviors of both parents in most of the families participating in their study, only 20% of children were actually “alienated” and only 6% were “severely alienated.” Even among the children who rejected a parent, all had multiple reasons for their hostility, including negative behaviors by the hated parent, such as child abuse or inadequate parenting, or the children’s own developmental or personality difficulties (Johnston, 2005; Johnston et al., 2005).

The fact that only a small fraction of children subjected to inter-parental hostilities and alienating conduct by their parents have been found to actually become “alienated” suggests that the focus on alienation is a tempest in a teapot – one that continues to distract from and undermine the accurate assessment of abuse and concomitant risks to children.

Lack of Evidence Base for Long-term Impact of Alienation

Johnston and others have acknowledged that “there is very little empirical data to back up their “clinical observations” that alienated children are significantly undermined in their emotional and psychological development. In fact, Johnston and Kelly (2004b) forthrightly state that “there are no systematic long-term data on the adjustment and well-being of alienated compared to non-alienated children so that long-term prognostications are merely speculative” (p. 84). And, contrary to the common assertions of evaluators and alienation theorists that alienation is a devastating form of emotional abuse of children, Judith Wallerstein, the groundbreaking researcher of divorce who first pointed out the problem of children’s sometimes pathological alignment with the custodial parent after divorce, found in her follow-up study that children’s hostility toward the other parent after divorce was in every case temporary, and resolved of its own accord, mostly within one or two years (Bruch, 2001; Wallerstein et al., 2000).

Perhaps the most disturbing misuse of PA is seen when PA adherents fail to distinguish between children who are estranged from a non-custodial parent due to abuse or other negative behavior from children who have been wrongly influenced by their favored parent to hate or fear the other. Thus, leading adherents to PA theory including Johnston and colleagues sometimes describe children's symptoms and psychological harms and attribute them to "alienation," while simultaneously acknowledging that their research shows that "alienated" children include those who are justifiably estranged due to the disfavored parent's conduct. Cases worked on by this author have shown that abused children display many of the symptoms that are frequently attributed to "alienation" both in the courts and in this literature (Compare Johnston, Walters, & Olesen, 2005; Johnston & Kelly, 2004b with Kathleen C. Faller, 1999; Righthand, 2003). Such discussions attribute to alienation harms which, in fact, may well be due to the disfavoured parent's own behaviours (Meier, 2010).

This failure to distinguish between whether harm to children – or their hostility to their father – is caused by alienation or abuse sets up a paradoxically disastrous dynamic: So long as an abuser can convince a court that the children's attitudes can be labelled "alienation," he can benefit from the very impact of his abuse. In Jordan v. Jordan, the trial court found (based on two alienation psychologists' testimony) that the older of two children was severely alienated from her father, who had been found to have twice committed intrafamily offenses against the mother. Therefore, the court ruled that the legislative presumption against joint custody to a batterer was rebutted – by the child's alienation, which, the court stated, would cause her emotional damage, and which it was presumed could best be cured by more time with her father (who she adamantly refused to see). The problem with this analysis was that neither the experts nor the judge considered the possibility that the child's "alienation" may have been at least in part a reaction to the father's violence toward the mother and in front of the child, as well as his known manhandling of the child herself. As a result, the father won joint (and eventually, sole) custody, even though the possibility that the child's hostility was a function of his own abusive behaviours was never ruled out (Jordan, 2010). When this argument was put before the Court of Appeals, that Court also ignored the fact that such reasoning makes battering a sure path to an award of custody – so long as the children become alienated as a result. The Court simply affirmed that the alienation label is sufficient grounds to rebut the presumption against custody to batterers, without regard to whether it is the batterer's own abuse which may have caused the child's "alienation" (Jordan, 2011).

It should be noted that, while alienation researchers do not discuss child witnessing of adult domestic violence as a form of emotional child abuse, research has unequivocally found that child witnesses to adult abuse can be profoundly negatively affected and/or traumatized, even if they are not themselves the direct target of physical or sexual violence (Lewis-O'Connor, Sharps, Humphreys, Gary, & Campbell, 2006; Bancroft & Silverman, 2012). Therefore, even where children have not been directly abused themselves, their fear or hostility toward the batterer of their mother may be entirely expected.

The fact that courts are not nuanced in applying alienation theory would not in itself be sufficient to indict the theory itself. However, discussions of PA within the scholarly literature supporting the concept demonstrate that these applications of the theory are quite consistent with the way it is understood by its researchers and theorists. For instance, while on the one hand conveying a more reasonable awareness of the many factors that contribute to a child's alienation from a parent, Johnston and collaborators continue to pathologize mothers whose children are hostile or afraid of their fathers. In some of their earlier work they even go so far as to pathologize the "aligned" parent who "often fervently believes that the rejected parent is dangerous to the child in some way(s): violent, physically or sexually abusive, or neglectful" (p. 258). They go on to describe the pursuit of legal protections and other means of assuring safety as a "campaign to protect the child from the presumed danger [which] is mounted on multiple fronts [including] restraining orders..." (p. 258). Finally, like Gardner, these purported rejectors of PAS continue to assert that a parent can "unconsciously" denigrate the other parent to the child "as a consequence of their own deep psychological issues" which cause them to "harbor deep distrust and fear of the ex-spouse..." (p. 257; see also Meier, 2010). This willingness to pathologize capable mothers even extends to mothers' "warm, involved" parenting – which they assert can powerfully fuel alienation in a child (Johnston et al., 2005, p. 208; Kelly and Johnston, 2001). Such discussions are more than sufficient to ensure that whenever a mother and child have ambivalence about the children's father, and certainly in most cases where mothers allege abuse, virtually any loving parenting by the mother can be labelled a form of "alienation."

In short, parental alienation as a theory has been built – not by scientific or empirical research, but by repeated assertions – at first more extreme assertions by Gardner, and now less extreme but still distorted assertions by more sophisticated psychological professionals. Unfortunately, it has been used virtually identically to PAS in family courts, to simply turn abuse allegations back against the protective parent and children. Anecdotal experience is now being confirmed by cutting edge research into "turned around" cases, i.e., those in which a court initially disbelieves a father is dangerous and, after some harm to the children, a second court corrects the error. Preliminary results of this research have identified PA labelling as one of three primary factors leading to

erroneous denials of an accused abuser (usually a father)'s dangerousness, and orders subjecting children to on-going abuse (Silberg, 2013; Silberg & Dallam, 2013). These preliminary results indicate that at least 37% of initial case errors (10 out of 27) were attributable to PA/PAS labeling. If an additional 12 cases in which the protective parent (usually a mother) was pathologized in similar manner (without the PA label) are included ,the percentage becomes 66%. Opinions of evaluators and Guardians Ad Litem (GALs) were a key factor in the court's unprotective erroneous decision in 67% of cases)
You can help prevent indoctrination and help your children resist alienation attempts by paying very close attention to your children's behavior toward you and by documenting everything you notice meticulously. If your high-conflict ex-spouse attempts to turn your children against you, you MUST bring it to the Court's attention as soon as possible. You will need the detailed documentation.

It may very well be the case that the judge does not take it seriously or doesn't know how to handle it. You may not have the experts lined up to prove the damage it's doing to your kids, but there's another important reason that you need to bring it out into the open—you need to be able to talk to your children about what is happening and you need to be able to counter the lies that are being told about you. Exposure and truth are the only way to begin to reverse this kind of indoctrination, and often it comes down to whether you can prove to your kids that they are being lied to—this is mind control, and your wife has gotten a head start.

More than likely your kids will think you are the one who is lying if you say anything that is contrary to what their mother has said. If you do not bring this to the Court's attention, you're taking a big risk if you talk to your kids about what's happening and start telling them the truth to counter the alienation. This is one more thing that could be used against you in court when your wife complains about YOU violating the court orders by talking to the kids and disparaging her.

2. Making Your Case. It is true that the legal system for the most part does not have the stomach to remove a child from the alienating parent he or she most closely identifies with, even though it's a very unhealthy alliance. It's also very, very difficult to prove alienation, and there is a lot of controversy about the concept. As a result, there is a tendency for judges to flat-out refuse to consider claims of alienation—in fact, the mere mention of the word "alienation" is usually enough to raise a judge's hackles. Claims of parental alienation are often viewed with suspicion and doubt because "parental alienation" has become a trendy catch-phrase that is sometimes used by parents as an excuse to avoid their responsibilities to their kids.

Talk the Talk

When making your case to a judge, unless it is a judge who is well known to be pro-active in cases of parental alienation, it's usually better to describe the problem in terms such as "the mother is lying to the children and instilling irrational fears about their father" or "the mother is unwilling to co-parent and is excluding the father from their lives" or "the mother is withholding the children during father's time with the children and is damaging their parent-child relationship." All of those descriptions paint a clearer picture than claiming that the mother is alienating the children from their father, which could mean almost anything.

Prove It

You will have to prove your case, and that will require more than just your word against the word of the kids' mother. This is where your documentation will play a vital role. If you have been documenting as they occur the behaviors of your children and your ex-wife, your journals should be admissible as evidence. The fact that you have consistently journaled about these events lends credibility to the testimony you're presenting to the judge. It will often be the case that you don't know exactly what your ex has said or done to cause the change in your children. In these cases, it's important that you document in detail what is going on with your children.

Pay particular attention to comments your children make that sound like they have been rehearsed or which sound awkward and unlike the type of things that children say spontaneously. For instance, if you tell your child that you look forward to seeing them on the weekend and your child says in response, "You're so irresponsible, you probably won't even pick me up" it's probably something your child has heard from their other parent. An 8-year old is not likely to spontaneously conclude that his father is "irresponsible" and would not describe it in those terms. If your child refers to you as "unstable," "abusive," "erratic," "labile," "narcissistic," "lazy," etc., those terms have likely been implanted through repetition by their other parent. Kids don't come up with these concepts on their own. Document the exact words that your child uses as well as the context in which these things are said. While journaling about these behaviours and attitudes of your children, note how the behaviours are different compared to a time before the alienation started and note the lack of any precipitating event that would give rise to these attitudes. Also note how it makes you feel as a parent

Be a Perfect Parent. Well, no one is perfect, right? But, especially while you're fighting this battle, you have to be as close to perfect as possible. That means don't ever miss your visitation and don't ever miss an opportunity to connect with your children. As long as you are not restrained from seeing them or placed on supervised visitation, you do not have to limit your contact to every other weekend or whatever your orders provide.

Establish a regular presence at the kids' schools because their mother will be smearing you to the teachers and school administrators; if those folks can observe for themselves that you're a loving, caring parent and not a hump-backed ogre, they cannot as easily be roped into believing lies about you. If they are called to testify in court, it will be hard for them to say negative things about you if they have their own positive experience of you.

Go have lunch with your kids at school; sneak them encouraging or silly notes in their lockers; send them cards in the mail; set up email accounts for them that their mother cannot access; purchase cell phones for the kids and keep their plans up to date so there is an open line of communication; be available and always put them first; don't be late picking them up; always keep your promises to them; be at every game, concert, recital, open house, etc.; show up at practices or rehearsals and get to know coaches and instructors. The more time you spend with them the better because when they are experiencing you live and in person on a regular basis, it will be harder for negative perceptions of you to take hold.

As tempting as it may be, do not talk negatively about their mother—particularly not in a spiteful or gratuitous way. That's not to say that you cannot correct lies their mother tells them, but you cannot just come out and call their mother a liar—it will be a conversation stopper. This kind of discussion with your children may best be handled with the help of a professional counsellor. Again, be careful about the professionals you choose because if you select someone who is not experienced in dealing with alienation issues, you could actually further the alienation process rather than alleviate it.

I typically recommend that clients participate with their children in family counselling when alienation has started to affect a child's attitude and behaviour toward the target parent. In that case, your child will have some irrational beliefs about you that you will probably find maddening. Communication will be difficult, and your child may refuse to even talk about it with you, in which case you should not force the issue—but you also cannot afford to drop the issue altogether. Get professional assistance to guide the conversations. You may find yourself feeling anger toward your child because behavior such as this hurts and feels like betrayal. It is not your child's fault and you cannot direct your anger at your child—this will further alienate him. Your child is being manipulated and controlled just like you were when you were married to the high-conflict woman.

Be aware of what you are telling yourself as this is happening. Too often, a target parent internalizes the rejection and buys into the distortions, believing that the child doesn't love him and doesn't want to be with him. I've seen a few dads give up on having a relationship with his kids—he stops insisting on visitation, he stays away from schools and sporting events out of shame and ultimately he loses any connection with his kids. This is devastating to children and to the alienated parents who love them. Do not give in to this kind of treatment!

It is not your authentic child who is rejecting you—it is a programmed, scripted Stepford child who needs help sorting things out. It's not fair, it hurts, it is stressful and demeaning, but if your child is being trained to fear or hate you, your child needs you to help him find his way back to a loving relationship. Do not help your crazy ex deprive your child of a loving relationship with you.

*Please note: Although we are speaking in this context of the mother being the alienating parent, this very sad phenomenon can be carried out equally effectively by either father or mother. I have seen it happen plenty of times on both sides, and it seems to be happening with increasing frequency while the courts and even behavioural health professionals lag behind in their understanding and ability to deal

And yeah those shells we found on the beach in South Carolina
Does the smell of a cottonwood tree ever remind you
Of those memories, of you and me, that I still see hope you got 'me all Girl I'm still waiting on life to begin again Still waiting on love to give a second chance To stop me and steal my breath the way you did I'm still looking for your Jeep in every parking lot Still taste your lips with every whiskey shot
And I hope you found whatever I am not found yet Because I feel like all my better days are gone Yes, I feel like all my better days are gone And I think you got 'me all Girl I think you got 'me all

Anger signals your body to prepare for a fight. This reaction is commonly classified as "fight or flight." When you get angry, adrenaline and other hormones are released into the bloodstream. Then your blood pressure goes up, your heart beats faster, and you breathe faster.
Many people mistakenly believe that anger is always a bad emotion and that expressing anger is not okay. In reality, anger can be a normal response to everyday events. It is the right response to any situation that is a real threat.

Anger can be a positive driving force behind our actions. Anger can also be a symptom of something else, depending on how often a person feels angry and how angry the person feels.

Hostility is being ready for a fight all the time. Hostile people are often stubborn, impatient, hotheaded, or have an "attitude." They are frequently in fights or may say they feel like hitting something or someone. Hostility isolates you from other people.

Anger and constant hostility keep your blood pressure high and increase your chances of having another health problem, such as depression, heart attack, or a stroke.

Teens who say they often feel angry and hostile also more often feel anxious, stressed, sad, and fatigued. They have more problems with alcohol and drug abuse, smoking, and eating disorders than teens who do not have high levels of anger.

Violent behavior often begins with verbal threats or relatively minor incidents, but over time it can involve physical harm. Violent behavior is very damaging, both physically and emotionally. Violent behavior can include physical, verbal, or sexual abuse of an intimate partner (domestic violence), a child (child abuse), or an older adult (elder abuse).

Violence causes more injury and death in children, teenagers, and young adults than infectious disease, cancer, or birth defects. Murder, suicide, and violent injury are the leading causes of death in children. Violence with guns is one of the leading causes of death of children and teenagers in the United States.

If you are angry or hostile or if you have violent behavior, it is important to find help. You can learn ways to control your feelings and actions.

If you have been abused or assaulted, contact your doctor as soon as possible. If you have questions about how soon you should be seen, you can check your symptoms. Hostility in children is a personality characteristic which causes great concern to parents, educators and others involved in child-rearing practices. There is much misunderstanding of the hostile and aggressive impulses of children and these characteristics are usually measured in terms of adult feelings. This monograph is the culmination of a study by a psychologist who attempted to scrutinize and examine the feelings of hostility in small children which was directed primarily against parents and parent-substitutes

. ONE OF MY most vivid memories from my childhood is walking in on my parents having a huge row in the kitchen.

This row, for me, signalled the end of their relationship and the beginning of the most difficult period of my life. As an only child, sadness and grief became my siblings when they separated.

Often during and after a relationship breakdown, parents are so caught up in their own hurt and fears, and the thoughts of being alone again, that they are oblivious of the impact their split has had on their children.

So how should parents deal with the aftermath of separation? Here are some tips:

1. Don’t diminish the impact.

I’ve seen parents convince themselves that their child will be OK, that the separation didn’t affect them and that life goes on.

If only this were true. Whether it’s visible or not, your child could be harbouring many hurtful feelings and unable to understand or process what’s happening.

Don’t minimise what has happened. Accept that damage might have been done and that your child will likely need time to process what has happened.

2. Deal with your guilt.

Feeling guilt over hurting your child is completely natural, but it’s important not to project your own guilt onto your child, be it through anger or overcompensating with excessive love.

All children need parents with healthy self-esteem and the traits associated with this, such as strong boundaries, clear expression and confidence in their ability.

Ask yourself why you are choosing to be so hard on yourself. Do you feel like you deserve love? Have you carried guilt around with you all your life? Could you have inherited it from your parents?

Rebuilding self-esteem involves prioritising your needs, looking after your body and surrounding yourself with healthy people who support your decision to end your relationship, despite having a child.

If the breakup is particularly nasty, you might face resistance from your ex-partner.

Jealously and resentment are commonplace and can be destructive for all parties involved in the split; it is important to detach from the hurt and stay focused on who you want to be.

3. Ensure your children are not carrying the burden.

I felt responsible for my parent's separation. I felt like it was my fault. I also felt I was responsible for their happiness. I worried about them constantly and I wanted to protect their feelings.

I took responsibility for something which didn't belong to me. A child CANNOT carry their parents. They CANNOT fix a marriage and it is NOT their job to make their parents feel good about themselves.

Your child needs to feel valued for who they are, not for what they do.

They will need to be reminded, preferably by both parents, that they are not responsible for what has happened – that each person is responsible for their own emotions and that nothing that has happened changes the fact that they are a special little person and deserve all the happiness in the world.

4. Remind them they have not been abandoned.

Watching my own father leave during the early stages of the separation created a sense of abandonment, a fear that he would never return.

This is something I carried with me right through to adult life. To be abandoned by a parent is an indescribable loss.

The child needs to know that they have not been left behind. That the parent will always be there for them and will never leave no matter what happens.

5. Express your emotions.

It's OK to be sad. It's OK to be angry. It's OK to be afraid. These are natural reactions to what has happened and your child should be allowed to express this. They should know it's OK to feel how they do and talk about it.

6. Fill the void.

It's important to surround your child with positive role models, be they male or female, who can see your child's potential, and demonstrate healthy behaviours and self-respect.

7. Park the bias.

One of my college lecturers once told me when working through a separation that a child will always side with the parent who DOESN'T speak badly of the other parent.

My mother never once spoke ill of my father as she knew this would not only be unfair on me but would only serve to deepen the wound further.

A young child is still emotionally bound to both parents, so to speak badly of one par

I was wondering if you could do a post about empathic limits. What is an appropriate response to bad behaviour from an unconditional parenting approach? For example, every time I come home with my daughter, I remind her that when we go inside she must take off her shoes. She often will immediately run to the couch and climb onto it with her shoes on. I know she does this precisely because she knows she's not supposed to, and now I warn her if she doesn't get down she will get a timeout. Usually she gets a timeout. I can't not respond when she does something like this. What can I do instead of a timeout?"

There is no such thing as a brat, only a child who is hurting. When our starting point as parents is a close bond with our children, we are their North Star, the point around which they orient. They want more than anything in the world to protect that relationship and meet our expectations. If our child is acting like a brat, she's either signalling that she needs a stronger connection with us, that she's got some big feelings she needs our help with, or that she can't meet our expectation without some tailored support

Setting empathic limits

Kids don't share our priorities. Why should they? They have their own priorities (jumping on the couch!) and no understanding of our world view (couches cost money). So it's our job, all day, every day, to guide them. "Shoes get the couch dirty...no shoes on the couch." The more firm and consistent you are, the more your child can accept your limit, grieve about it, and move on. The more empathic you are, the more your child will accept your limits without needing to rebel against them. Redirection is the best way to stop the behavior because it channels the energy. "I see that's so much fun! And you know the couch is not for jumping. Come, off the couch. Let's go jump on the old mattress in the basement."

All kids will naturally test limits to see if they're firm. That means for now you'll need to stay with her as you enter the house and helping her get

But what if she darts away from you and makes a beeline for the couch, before you can get her shoes off? She's sending you a signal that something's getting in the way of her cooperating with you. What? Emotions. Kids store up their feelings, waiting for a safe chance to release them with a compassionate witness. That's you. If you get to the bottom of these tangled emotions, you'll stop "bad" behavior before it starts.

Sure, you can make her "stuff" those feelings, by screaming at her or punishing her. She'll comply, eventually--until she's old enough to rebel. The teen years won't be pretty. Her chances of depression or anxiety go way up. And you'll never be as close as you could be, to this person you brought into the world.

Or you can help her with those feelings. It will help her cooperate with your agenda. It will teach her emotional intelligence. It will make her more able to meet your expectations as she gets older. And it will bring you closer. How? Play when you can. Cry when you have to.

7. Help the child with the feelings that are keeping him from cooperating: Play when you can.

Take a deep breath and repeat after me: "It is not an emergency. We can play with this." Keep your tone light and playful, so you get her giggling. "Excuse me?! Are you on that couch with your shoes on?! We'll see about that! I'm the couch protector, and I always get my girl!" Scoop her up, laughing, and toss her over your shoulder. As you run around the house with her, take her shoes off and drop them. Sing a silly chant about how much you love her and you'll never let her go. Keep dropping her on the couch and scooping her up again. Finally, collapse together on the couch for a good snuggle.

The next time you enter the house, before you go in the door, tell her you want to play the game again, but first she has to take her shoes off with you, right inside the door. Transform the game into one of re-connection and celebration. Use it any time you need to interrupt "bad" behavior. Giggling releases upset feelings just as crying does, and it triggers oxytocin, t

Bullying is all about power, really - bullies like to feel in control of the social situation, so they try to obliterate anyone they find unsettling or problematic in any way.

And yet many of our greatest leaders have been motivated by a high need for power, so not everyone who is attracted to power is a potential bully. Qualities such as moral engagement, courage, tolerance and compassion are the traits that distinguish great leaders from brutal bullies, and these are the traits that parents should try to cultivate in their power-crazy kids. Not only because the parent will be helping their child to become a leader who might go on to be inspirational, but, more importantly, because the pain and destruction that mindless bullying causes to both children and adults is profound.

Every day, some schoolchildren eat their lunch in toilet cubicles in fear of bullies; others spend their entire break and lunch hanging around their lockers because there is no one to hang out with; countless kids immediately panic when they hear the familiar ping from their mobile and they realise that yet another so-called friend has posted spiteful venom about them on social media. It is relentless, and it is deeply damaging.

Kids are usually targeted by bullies because they stand out for some reason. It is a natural stage of the adolescent's development to become preoccupied with their inclusion into the social group, and so, as a result, many teenagers become rabidly cliquey. This is why they feel unsettled by anyone who stands out from the herd, by the kids who are visually different or have certain characteristics, or a strong personality that isn't easily assimilated into the narrow confines of teenage life.

If you look around any group of people, you will see the quiet, passive types; the loud, dominant types; the easy-going, conforming types, and the ones who are different in some way. Usually (although sadly, not always) adults don't pick on easy prey - most of us have learnt to be better than that - but teenage bullies and their sidekicks often haven't yet matured enough to care about the impact of their behaviour. Parents can help their children by building their self-awareness and by learning how their children might need to handle their environment, if they are to survive adolescence without attracting the attention of a potential bully.

In early childhood, socialising is relatively easy; whoever is nearby and whoever likes the same things are considered the child's 'friends'. Very little is asked of these so-called friends - all that is required, really, is that the child shows up, learns to share (sometimes) and doesn't hit their friends.

In middle childhood, friendship becomes a little more complex, as children at this age wish to play by the rules, and so they expect reciprocity from their friends - it's all about 'you do this for me and I'll do that for you' at this stage. Many kids this age also haven't yet developed the social skills to know how to handle more than one or two friends at the same time, so play dates tend to be easier if there is only one friend invited over. This is one reason why children at this age become very fond of secret clubs - it is an interesting (if a bit self-absorbed) way to reduce the number of friends they have to deal with at any given time.

It isn't a very nice experience for the children who are being excluded, but funnily enough, many kids are used to the ruthless straight-talking that is common in middle childhood, and it is often the parents who are more upset by the events than the kids. Having a best friend and being joined at their hip is another way to simplify the friendships in your life. Best friends suit many children at this age - especially girls who particularly enjoy connecting on an emotional level - because then the child can focus all their personality on one person, and pretty much disregard the rest of the world.

It is when children become tweens and teens that friendships often become more demanding, complex and, sadly, fraught with difficulties. There have been countless studies of cliques among children and, from the age of 11 years old and upwards, certain hierarchies have been identified in the typical classroom.

Approximately one-third of students tend to be in the dominant popular group. This group or clique is the most powerful group, and those who have a high need for power will often seek to be included in this group. This is the clique who may engage in a lot of strategic behaviour because of their desire to maintain or enhance their social status. About one-tenth of children are in the 'wannabe' group. These kids hang around the edges of the popular group, hoping desperately to get the nod so they can join the cool clique. They usually get enough crumbs of approval from the head table to keep them hooked, but they rarely gain full acceptance.

About half of students occupy the middle ground. This involves smaller, independent friendship groups, where the emphasis is on being loyal, kind and supportive of each other. These kids often dislike the popular kids, because they see them as unfriendly, political and standoffish, but they also look down on the less popular kids. About one-tenth of the students are socially isolated from every group. These children are most at risk of being targets of bullying, and these are the children that need more support from family so that they can emerge from their childhood with their sense of self intact.

Children are targeted for a wide variety of reasons - it isn't only difference, but the fact that they are easy prey that can put them on the bully's radar. Quiet and passive personalities are unlikely to stand up to the bully's mob, and so they can be targeted when the bullies feel the need for a quick shot of power.

Richard was an ordinary, quiet boy with a couple of good friends until one day, at the end of first year in school, there was some horseplay when he was getting changed after swimming, and his shorts came down in the midst of it all. From then on, Richard was called 'Little Dick' by his classmates, and his life was irrevocably transformed from that single event.

The whole thing took a life of its own. Looking back on it, Richard believes he should have immediately let loose, defended himself, told his parents, told the teachers and surrounded himself with support. But instead, quite understandably, he stayed silent, he kept his head down and desperately hoped that the slagging would die out.

It didn't.

The girls heard about Richard's new nickname, and soon it became the joke of the year among his schoolmates. Puerile, nasty and low it might have been - but bored teenagers looking for a cheap shot of power will do almost anything for a laugh. And so, if you have a quiet, passive child who is moving into a new environment, extra c It can also be helpful if the parents help their child to reignite old friendships - although, for more introverted kids, creating a space for your child and you to connect regularly can be more supportive than adding to their social calendar. Maybe go for a hot chocolate every Friday or something similar, so that there are regular opportunities to reflect on small worries as they arise. Then, when a problem crops up, the parents will already know the subtleties of the situation and can give some much-needed perspective on the issue.

Connection is the royal road to having a good relationship with your teenagers - teens don't tend to want to communicate with parents because, at this stage in their lives, friendships are often more important than anything else. However, if you can regularly connect with your teenager, they will be more likely to turn to you in times of crisis. It could be over a shared love of rom-coms or it could be your favourite soccer team; it really doesn't matter how you connect; what matters is the deeper feelings of belonging and connection.

This is the first generation of kids who have been raised with social media, and the impact of this has yet to be identified. However, you wouldn't need a master's in psychology to figure out that the relentless selfies, the stylised photos showing off perfect lives, and the obsession with counting your 'likes' is likely to lead to a generation that are more self-absorbed, narcissistic and, ironically, more disconnected than previous generations.

Just recently, five teenagers in Florida allegedly filmed a man drowning in a pond. They sniggered, they mocked and they watched him die. It is alleged that not one of them reported the incident, phoned the emergency services or tried to help in any way. Jamel Dunn's body was found at the bottom of the pond five days later.

These kids, sneering and jeering at a man who was dying, were so self-absorbed, so utterly disconnected from themselves and out of touch with their humanity that, if the circumstances were different, you would almost feel sorry for them.

As a psychotherapist, I am often quietly appalled by the bullying behaviour that is casually described by the teenagers I meet. The utter disdain that teenagers often have for the 'loners' and 'freaks' in their social domain is chilling. It's nearly always done 'just for the laugh', but it's seldom funny - it's usually degrading and cruel.

When I challenge these otherwise considerate and kind kids, they tend to look bemused, shrug their shoulders and mindlessly dismiss the pain of their peers. In my book, Bully-Proof Kids, I attempt to bring the bystanders in from the edges of the drama and place them slap-bang in the centre of it all. Bystanders are the people who see everything but do nothing. Millions of kids today are bystanders to cruel bullying, to controlling friendships and to power plays between stronger and weaker personalities. They let bullying happen. Yet, without a gallery to play to, bullying loses its fizz and, as the writer William Burroughs says: "There are no innocent bystanders... what are they doing there in the first place?"

The bystanders are the silent majority, and they hold the majority of the power. It is estimated that bystanders are present in 90pc of cases of bullying, and they can often stop the bullying within 10 seconds if they choose to intervene. The good news is that if we can create a culture of upstanders who are ready to stand in the path of bullies, then we will significantly reduce the impact, the frequency and the duration of bullying. The bad news is that bystanders, by their very nature, seldom wish to raise their head above the parapet.

This is why parents and schools need to join forces and help provide a culture of upstanding; parents need to stop demanding that the schools magic the bullying away, and the schools need to stop underplaying the bullying. I work as a psychotherapist in a private practice in rural Ireland and, of the three second-level schools in the area, one of the schools appears to handle bullying very effectively; another does reasonably well; while the third school encounters bullying on an almost continuous basis.

It is remarkable because these schools are similar, and the kids are from mostly comparable backgrounds. The difference is that the school with the bullying problem minimises any incidents of bullying or pretends that there is no bullying taking place at all, while the other two schools are, to a greater or lesser extent, willing to address the problem and take necessary steps to deal with it.

Teenagers these days all too often feel embattled, insecure and mentally all over

The clinical psychologist and parenting expert advises on the best approach to deal with a demanding five-year-old and coping with a new partner's adult children who won't acknowledge you.

Question: My five-year-old boy has, in recent times, become very demanding. He wants to get his own way and get everything first, such as treats or use of the iPad.

He is also competitive and always wants to win at board games or football and gets angry when he loses.

When he wins, he shouts "I won, I am the winner".

When he is corrected, or does not get his own way, he gets angry and could grab things and throw them. Or he might hit and kick those near him.

We are at our wits' end with him. Have you any ideas about how to deal with all of this?

David replies: Your son sounds like he needs a firm hand to guide him, and lots of understanding about the fact that he gets frustrated and cross when things don't go his way. There are lots of things about his behaviour that are very normal for a five-year-old.

Out of interest, I wonder if your son started school this year? The wider social mix of school can often be the prompt for children to increase their competitiveness, boastfulness and challenging of rules. Maybe other children have influenced some of the behaviour you now see.

I often think that one of the most important lessons that children have to learn is that they are not the centre of the known universe and that they don't wield all of the power in their family.

The key to teaching children that you have the power and the authority, and that they must accommodate to your desires more than you will accommodate to theirs, lies in being firm, really consistent, and kind about imposing your will. I am not surprised to hear that your son is demanding, or that he insists on coming first, or winning any game that he is part of. Small children can't bear losing, because they can't cope with the disappointment that follows.

Learning to lose graciously is a real skill. It is also a lesson that needs lots of repetition. We come to learn it by losing to people who win graciously.

Unlike your son, who lords it over everyone when he does win, gracious winners are delighted with their own victory but compassionate to those that they have beaten.

Your son requires lots of correction when he is involved in games. He needs to be coached in the social etiquette of enjoying his win, but realising that others might be sad about their loss.

Similarly, he needs to play games where he loses, and where his loss is greeted with understanding about the great disappointment or feelings of dejection, disillusionment or frustration that things didn't go the way he wanted.

In order to learn to win and lose graciously, children need experience of both. They need adults around them who can help them to soothe and regulate the strong feelings of elation and upset that might come depending on the outcome.

Your approach to all the other disappointments or frustrations that he experiences, when he is told "no", or is told he "must" do something, needs to be similar. You need to be firm in insisting that the particular limit or rule is upheld and consistent in enforcing the limit.

Dealing with his aggression requires equal consistency and firmness. He needs to realise that you won't let him hit or kick you. That means moving out of his range, or moving him to a place where he can't actually get at anyone.

As you move him, you can be understanding about his frustration, but definitive about the fact that even though he is upset, he may not hurt anyone else.

All too often, we tell small children to stop hitting us, saying things like, "Stop! That hurts mammy, you are making me sad". But equally often, we then don't prevent our child (who is still small enough to lift out of harm's way) from hitting.

As well as the verbal command to "Stop!" we need to use a bit of physical intervention to ensure they are not in a position to continue to hit us, by, for example, moving them out of the way or to a safer place out of reach.

Firmness, kindness, understanding and consistency are the best ways to deal with frustrated five-year-olds.

My new partner's adult children won't acknowledge me. It is awkward and upsetting for everyone

Question: I have just begun a relationship with a new partner. He has been married and recently separated, while my husband died two years ago. I've no children of my own. My new partner has three grown-up kids, aged 18, 21 and 22. It's like I don't exist for them. They refuse to acknowledge me. His youngest daughter comes to visit occasionally, but she actually looks through me and will leave a room if I enter. He has asked her what the problem is and she won't tell him. It makes family gatherings very awkward. Have you any ideas?

David replies: Despite the joy of finding love again, after separation or bereavement, it can often be very difficult when people enter into new relationships where there are children from a previous relationship.

It does help when you don't take those children's feelings towards you, or their behaviour towards you, personally. It might help you to understand things from their perspective. When we do, their apparent rejection of us - the 'new' partner - may make more sense. Lots of children worry about the impact a new relationship will have on their own relationship with their parent. Many fear a dilution of the love from their father or mother.

Your partner's youngest daughter may have been the 'apple of his eye'. While he

Having found love again, with you, her dad may now appear all-consumed in this new relationship. His daughter may feel that he is distracted from her and her needs. Worse, from her perspective, she may even feel that he has chosen you over her.

Another difficulty for children (even adult children) when their parent begins a new relationship is that it underlines the ending of the old relationship.

So in your case, your partner's children may in fact have suddenly been hit by the reality of their own parents' separation and the fact that their dad and mum are no longer together.

The pain that then comes with the realisation of the loss can be massive and deeply felt. Alongside the despair and sadness that it can bring comes, often, anger.

If children want an outlet to express that anger then who better to direct it towards than the person who they may perceive 'stole' their father from their mother?

It makes sense, too, that your partner's daughter would be reluctant to talk to him about whatever her reasons are for her dislike of, or distrust in, you.

If she is openly critical of you in any way, then he may argue with, withdraw from, or punish her in some way for this. She risks jeopardising her relationship with her dad further by complaining or expressing dissatisfaction with his life-choices.

She may feel it is easier to be passively aggressive by ignoring you, because it is very hard to challenge her in a concrete manner when she is disengaged like this. There may come a time to challenge this kind of behaviour, but that time has not yet arrived.

For now, because your relationship with your partner is relatively new, the most important thing you can do is to be patient and understanding with all of his children. Even though they are adults, they still need time to adjust to the new situation.

Maybe this means giving them space and time with their dad during these early stages of your relationship with him, when you are not around.

They need time to realise that you are not a threat to them, that you are not the cause of their parents' break-up and that their parents are indeed now separated for good.

You may also need to be patient with their dad too. He, like them, needs to process the complex mix of emotions that comes with his new circumstances. He may want to please everyone, which is rarely possible!

He may be delighted to have found love, with you, but may be confused, or upset, by the complexities it has created in his relationships with his children. Time and understanding will, hopefully, make everything easier.

I cannot cope with my teenage son. He is my youngest, aged 14, with an older brother and sister, both in their early 20s, who have happy, successful, independent lives and with whom I have a lovely relationship. At home there's me, my son and my husband, who has been in my son's life since he was four. My son is popular and doesn't struggle at school. We were incredibly close as mother/son relationships go.

I was not married to his father. When we split I took only the children; he kept the house and failed to pay maintenance until the children were older, when he remarried. His wife is lovely; my husband and I babysit their new baby.

My youngest son has hit the teenage years but it's different from his siblings, most notably in the way he compares me with his father so unfavourably. His dad is the party man, not worrying about homework or bedtimes, letting our son be out at all hours and indulging him. My son hardly interacts with us at home, saying I am horrible, he doesn't like me, and that he lives with me only out of convenience. His dad, however, is "amazing" and I could learn from him.

I usually grit my teeth, but recently I cracked and shouted unforgivable things – such as his father not being there for parents' evenings, sports days, sick days. To be despised in such an outright way is breaking me. I am ashamed I bad-mouthed his father, but I was sick of hearing how great he is. I fear I will do this again and need help to cope more appropriately.

Your son is saying he doesn't like you, but it isn't that simple. I consulted child and adolescent psychotherapist Ruth Glover (childpsychotherapy.org.uk), who agreed with you that having had a close mother/son relationship makes the "hatred" feel harder to bear (though it will make things better in the long run). Glover thought you might be struggling with the fear of "losing your last child, and thus your sense of being a mother".

I wondered how accurate your memory is of life with your older two children? Did the fact you still had your youngest at home when they were going through this stage cushion the blows of *their* adolescence?

Adolescence can be a time when "anything not quite worked through in the early years can resurface", Glover said. So things that happened years ago, that you think they weren't bothered about, can suddenly rear their heads. It's also a time when it's essential that children start to discover themselves and begin to separate from their parents. "Otherwise," Glover said, "they would never want to leave home."

Your son may have noticed his dad has not been there at times, and this may have led to him feeling unwanted. "He may," Glover said, "be making you feel rejected, because that's how he's feeling."

Children "throw out" uncomfortable feelings they cannot process (adults do this, too). They project them on to adults, often picking a "safe bet" adult – in this case you – over one they feel isn't so reliable (his dad).

And the new baby is significant. "The timing of the baby, coinciding with his own early adolescent struggle with identity and where he fits, may be hard for your son." He may also fear that his dad will reject him again for the baby.

I asked Glover if what you said in your outburst was so very wrong. "It's understandable and OK to show you have limits," she said. "Your son may have been pushing for you to say those things. He probably knew them already and was struggling. And then you've reinforced what he already feels."

I'm 17 and my parents control me and want me to conform – what can I do?

Read more

But don't panic! Try to find a good time to tell him you are sorry for what you said (maybe while you are driving, so you are not face to face in a confrontational way) and you can see he's angry – though he may want to think about the things he said, too. You don't need to say more than that.

Glover wondered whether there was traction in "working with his dad, trying to talk to him away from your son". But he may not want to help and may enjoy the division. It's likely, thought Glover, "that your son is idealising his relationship with his dad, because it doesn't feel very stable".

When you start to lose your temper, remind yourself that he's trying to communicate how he feels by making other people feel the same way.

At this critical time...

... for our natural world, our societies and our media, The Guardian is committed to a different model for open, independent journalism – sustained through generous reader support. When progressive ideals are being challenged by those in power across the globe, we're dedicated to investigating with courage and reporting with honesty. But we need your ongoing support to keep working as we do.

The Guardian will engage with the most critical issues of our time – from the escalating climate catastrophe to widespread inequality to the influence of big tech on our lives. At a time when factual information is a necessity, we believe that each of us, around the world, deserves access to accurate reporting with integrity at its heart.

Our editorial independence means we set our own agenda and voice our own opinions. Guardian journalism is free from commercial and political bias and not influenced by billionaire owners or shareholders. This means we can give a voice to those less heard, explore where others turn away, and rigorously challenge those in power.

We need your support to keep delivering quality journalism, to maintain our openness and to protect our precious independence. Every reader contribution, big or small, is so valuable Family It's adolescence. Stupid teen brains like we've all had saying and doing stupid stuff, which we regret when we're old enough to know better. Disengage emotionally and ignore the rages rather than react - one of the best mothers I know calls it the "bored policeman" approach. It's the only way to stop it becoming a battle and turning it back into what it really is - an expression of overreactive and impotent rage and juvenile incomprehension. Your son clearly was traumatised by the marriage split and the apparent rejection by his dad. He is feeling unloved and trying to push you away as a test e.g. if you really love him you will stay, if you don't you will go as well. He is doing this subconsciously. He is big in body but 14 year old boys are still children and still very insecure and emotional.
2- You should not have bad mouthed his father. But don't feel bad about shouting or getting annoyed, he clearly is pushing your buttons. Just try to be calm and when you are pushed beyond your limits, dont bad mouth, just tell him off for being rude and give him a consequence.
3- Congratulations on being mature enough to get on with the new wife, sadly many people are not so mature and rip their families apart by refusing to talk to the new one etc

There's a presumption that, unless the contrary is shown, the involvement of both parents in the child's life will further the child's welfare. Currently there's no definition of what 'involvement' is; this can include direct or indirect contact with the child."

However, after separation there's also no presumption that a child's time will – or should – be split equally between the parents and that the child/children will live with the mother rather than the father. Robinson says legal advice can help with negotiations about contact, and for out-of-court dispute resolution, such as mediation, to reach a contact agreement.

If agreement can't be reached, either parent may issue an application for a Child Arrangements Order which states who a child lives and has contact with.

"It's disappointing that so many fathers still think they've lost their rights regarding their children on separation. This is simply not the case," stresses Robinson.

"Timing is important. A parent who is isn't being allowed by the other parent to see their children should take action swiftly, to minimise the risk of the children suffering emotional harm from the loss of the relationship."

Parents with PR have the right to be consulted about the major decisions in their child's life, such as if the other parent wants to take the child out of the country. So if the child/children live with their mother after their parents' divorce, and she wants to take them on holiday abroad, she'd need the consent of her ex-husband and everyone else who has PR for the children.

Another example of where consent would be needed from others with PR for the child is if one parent wants to change a child's name. If consent from those with PR can't be obtained, a parent may need to apply for a Specific Issue Order to gain the court's permission.

If you're the parent wanting to stop the other party taking the child abroad, you can be proactive and apply to the court for an order that prohibits the other parent from doing so. This is known as a Prohibited Steps Order and depending on the circumstances of the case, you may need to make the application on an urgent basis, explains Robinson.

“We’ve seen a rise in the number of clients who have been stopped at the airport when trying to take their children out of the country, so taking a letter signed by the other parent is a wise precaution,” she adds.

After divorce or separation, a parent may wish to move away with the child/children. The relocation would be considered as either an internal relocation (i.e. a move to somewhere in the country), or an international relocation.

Robinson explains that, if an internal relocation is a substantial distance away and will involve the children moving schools, a parent will need the consent of the other parent with PR, and anyone else who has PR, or a court order if consent can’t be obtained.

If the proposed move is abroad, she says the written consent of everyone with PR will again be required. If the proper consent isn’t obtained, a parent may be committing a criminal offence, and Robinson says that because of how serious this can be, legal advice should be sought to ensure a parent has secured the correct consent.

Robinson adds: “Due to the time it can take for the court to determine an application to relocate, the application should be made in plenty of time before the intended move, otherwise you could easily find your plans have to be placed on hold before the court reaches a decision.”

The analysis of 6,000 children born in the UK at the turn of the century found that those whose parents move apart between the age of seven and 14 are significantly more likely - 16 per cent - to suffer emotional and behavioural problems than those whose parents stay together.

However, there was no difference between children aged between three and seven whose parents divorced and those of the same age who did not.

The University College London scientists behind the new research believe divorce is more damaging to adolescents than to younger children because they are more socially sensitive and better able to pick up on negative relationship dynamics.

The team examined reports of children's mental health at three, five, seven, 11 and 14, including emotional problems such as feelings of low mood and anxiety, and behavioural issues such as disobedience.

They compared information on children who experienced a family split with those who did not a fifth of children in the study saw their parents separate between the ages of 3 and 14.

Among older children, increased emotional problems were noticed for both boys and girls, but more severe behavioural issues were observed only in boys.

The study also shows that, after a family break-up, children from m more privileged backgrounds were just as likely to have mental health problems as their less advantaged peers.

Professor Emla Fitzsimons, who co-authored the study, said: "With adolescent mental ill-health a major concern nationally, there's a pressing need to understand the causes.

She added that, as well as a greater sensitive to relationship dynamics, older children are more likely to be affected by a family breakup than younger children because of disruption to schooling and friendships is often greater.

Published in the journal, Social Science and Medicine, the study also investigated the impact of the break-up on the mothers' mental health and financial resources.

Across the UK, women accounted for 90 per cent of lone parents, and most children in the study lived with their mothers after a split.

Mothers reported, on average, more mental health problems than those still with their partners if they separated when their children were older.

This is believed to be because the financial impact of divorce was greater the later on in the marriage.

According to the Office For National Statistics, there were 101,669 divorces of heterosexual couples in 2017, representing a 4.9 per cent decrease compared with 2016 but similar to the numbers of 2015.

Just over four in 10 marriages in the UK end in divorce.

Last year David Gauke, the Justice Secretary, announced an intention to allow no-fault divorces.

Under a simplified system, spouses would lose the ability to block a divorce as there would be no need for their husband or wife to prove adultery, unreasonable behaviour or desertion in a contested divorce.

It followed a high-profile Supreme Court ruling which ordered a wife to stay in her "loveless" marriage after her husband of 40 years denied that he had behaved unreasonably.

We have all heard in recent times about the changing face of modern Ireland. Many of us will know of couples who have gone through the trauma of separation and I am acutely aware of the increased support that families need in time of difficulty. But what about the children of these families? Government, through the National Children's Strategy, promised that children's lives will be better understood. Nowhere is that promise more important than in the whole area of parental separation. The publication of Children's Experiences of Parental Separation is one of the most anticipated events since the Government's Families Research Programme was first launched in 1999. The study, which was supported by the Department of Social and Family Affairs, deals with the experience of sixty children, aged between eight and seventeen years, most of whose parents had separated within the last five years. The study set out to gain an understanding, from children's perspectives, of the impact of parental separation on their lives and the support needs that arise from these experiences. The summary of the findings will make a major contribution to the debate about the separation of couples, the consequences for their children and how their lives can best be supported and enhanced. I was struck by the findings that children differed in their experiences of parental separation and that consequently it was not possible to conclude that separation was either a positive or a negative experience. However, patterns of shared feelings and perspectives were identified and The number of separated couples in Ireland is increasing, and public concern is growing about the consequences for children who experience this kind of change in their family life. The present study explores the experience of parental separation for children aged 8-17. The aim of the study was to describe how parental separation affects children's lives, from their own perspectives, including their views and feelings about the changes that occur in their everyday lives, such as at school, at home, and in their relationships with parents and other family members. Another aim was to discover what sort of support children experienced and needed, and the strategies they used to cope with the changes in their family life. METHODS The study used a qualitative approach to explore children's perspectives on their parents' separation. Individual interviews were conducted with 60 children – 36 girls and 24 boys – most of whose parents had separated within the previous five years. The ages of the children at the time of the separation ranged from 2 to 10 years, with an average age of 8 years. Children were contacted through schools and a range of agencies. 67% of the children had attended support services in connection with their parents' separation. None of the children said that they had directly experienced court proceedings, and only two children mentioned court involvement in the separation. For the purposes of data analysis, two age groups were created: 8-11 years ('younger children') and 13-17 years ('older

It is important for children to receive reassurances from parents that they were concerned about their children's well-being and committed to being available for them. • Communication between parents and children about the separation was highly important for all children, but especially adolescents. Children who were able to understand their parents' decisions or behaviour were better able to adapt to these family changes. • Communication was important not only at the time of separation, but over time, as families underwent further change, such as the addition of new family members, and as children themselves grew and changed. • Children whose non-resident parent had left suddenly and without explanation were particularly confused and distressed. • The large majority of children said that they had not been consulted about family arrangements concerning custody and visits with non-resident parents. Many did not want to be asked to make such major decisions. Reactions to parental separation • Children typically reacted to their parents' separation with a mix of negative and positive feelings, often felt simultaneously, for example sadness and relief. • Most children felt that separation was the best solution for their family, given the relationship difficulties between their parents. • Many children had a strong sense of being different from other children, and felt embarrassed to talk abut their parents' separation. • Many children were worried about the implications of the separation, both immediate and long-term. Some were worried about their parents' well-being. • Some children were concerned about parents developing relationships with new partners. However, children tended to have strong expectations that their non-resident parent (usually their father) would continue to play the role of parent, in spite of any further changes. There are positive things separating parents can do to minimise the negative impact of marital breakdown on children. Children vulnerable at this time, devoice but also resilient. Parents may be upset or angry while going through separation, but they are nearly always well-intentioned towards their children too.

The chain of events from parental conflict to separation and divorce can have a devastating impact on children and extended families as well as on the parents themselves. In addition, separation can bring other stressful occurrences, such as house moves, money problems, legal battles and loss of supportive relationships. Children can suffer a range of emotional and social difficulties. However, a significant number of children cope relatively well and, with the help of their parents, go on to lead happy lives after separation. How children cope largely depends on how their parents manage their split. Here are some suggestions about how to make the process less painful.

1 Take steps to manage your own stress to ensure you are coping personally During the course of a separation it is normal to experience a rollercoaster of emotions from upset and rage to guilt and shame. Many parents understandably become preoccupied with their own concerns before and after a separation. Your children really need you at this time, but the first step to helping them is to make sure you yourself are coping. Take whatever steps are necessary to get the support you need, be it counselling or a support group or confiding in a close friend.

2 Work constructively with your former partner on parenting issues One of the biggest things that damages children in a family is witnessing or suffering the effects of ongoing conflict between their parents. (Some children actually do better after parental separation if the new arrangement leads to less conflict and a more harmonious family environment.) For this reason, it is crucial that you work hard to develop a constructive relationship with your children's other parent. This is the single biggest factor that will help your children cope.

The more you can agree living and contact arrangements amicably and focus on your children's interests, the better it will be for them. A good way to do this is to develop a businesslike relationship with your former spouse; your aim is to move on from past hurts and to work constructively together as co-parents.

3 Help your children cope with divided loyalty It is very common for children to experience a divided loyalty between their parents. Make sure to give your children a balanced, fair and age-appropriate account of the separation and how it happened, and reassure them that both their parents still love them. Ideally, this message should be given by both parents, together or separately, and repeated many times.

Speak positively about your ex-partner in front of the children, or, if you feel this is not honest, make it clear that your negative feelings are your own and allow your children to feel differently. Don't communicate through your kids or use them as a go-between. If you need to discuss something with their other parent, do so directly.

4 Listen to your children and focus on their best interests and needs Children cope differently with their parents' separation, depending on their age and personality. Listen carefully to your children individually to understand what support they need. Even children who appear to be coping fine need special understanding. A good idea is make sure you have one-to-one time with your kids. Periodically raise the topic of the separation and ask them what they think and feel about it, how they are coping. As they get older they will have further questions and thoughts. Work hard at keeping the lines of communication open.

5 Minimise the moves and changes in your child's life after separation Sometimes the major losses in children's lives are not directly due to the separation itself. Often they are related to the other changes the children experience, such as moving house, leaving a school, losing friends because of a move, or not seeing grandparents as often. While parents often feel they need a fresh start after separation, research seems to suggest that children need the opposite.

Try to maintain as many of the good things in your children's life as you can. This might mean making a special effort to ensure they keep in contact with grandparents or relatives from the other side of the family, or arranging things so that they can stay in the same school and see the same friends.

Dr John Sharry answers parenting questions in the *Irish Times* Health + Family supplement each Tuesday; he is also codeveloper of the Parents Plus: Parenting When Separated course (parentsplus.ie/ separation) and author of the new book *Parenting When*

ana divorced her husband in 1999. Her ex, Jim, had been diagnosed with Narcissistic Personality Disorder and he has made Dana and their children's lives miserable for 14 years. Due to the long, drawn out legal battle and Jim's emotional abuse before and since the divorce, Dana was recently diagnosed with Post Traumatic Stress Disorder. She is being treated as an inpatient and discussed what life has been like for her over the last few years.

"I feel as if I've been in the middle of a war zone for an extended period of time. I've lived with daily fear for years; there has been no relief because some sort of conflict with my ex was always lurking around the corner," Dana says. "I didn't have time to process one event before I was dealing with another one."

"When divorced from someone like my ex, you don't have time to stop, process your feelings, grieve and move on," she continued. "You have to have your guard up at all times, be focused and ready for what is coming next and you learn quickly that there will be something coming."

Post-traumatic stress disorder is a normal emotional and psychological reaction to trauma (a painful or shocking experience) that exists outside of someone's normal life experiences.

According to the National Institute of Mental Health people who experience a traumatic event will react with shock, anger, nervousness, fear, or even guilt. For most people, these common reactions go away over time, but for someone experiencing PTSD, these feelings continue to escalate until the person has difficulty living a normal life. Someone with PTSD usually has symptoms for longer than a month and cannot function as well as they did before the traumatic event.

"It's like I'm constantly in survival mode," Dana says. "I perceive a lot of things as a threat. My reaction is immediate defense for survival. My reaction to an unexpected tap on the shoulder from behind is quite different from someone without PTSD. I jump, scream or run as if I'm under attack. It is hard to explain but everything feels like an attack on my safety or security. A car turned in front of me one day, there was plenty of room, no danger of the car hitting me but I froze. I was unable to drive ahead, could only sit and cry. I've lost myself and my ability to calm myself after even the smallest adrenaline rush."

Symptoms of PTSD are often grouped into three main categories that include:

Reliving the traumatic experience: Survivors of trauma may experience nightmares or flashbacks of the traumatic event. This might be triggered by something that reminds the survivor of the event, like the anniversary of the event or a similar location or even a language.

Avoidance: People may remove themselves from people or situations that are similar in some way to the traumatic event. Survivors may become detached from their loved ones and lose interest in their previous passions.

Increased arousal: Those with PTSD may become more sensitive to their emotions or bodily sensations. They may have high anxiety levels, insomnia, trouble focusing and be hyper-vigilant (always on guard), among other symptoms.

"I'm constantly under some kind of pressure," Dana says. "I'm not the same happy, loving person I once was. It feels like there's a barrier wall in front of me and I can't scale it."

Recovering from PTSD is a process and differs for each survivor. The goal for PTSD treatment is to reduce the physical and emotional symptoms as well as improve the survivor's ability to interact fully with their everyday life.

"First and foremost is some kind of personal conversation, talking or psychotherapeutic relationship," Dr. Arthur S. Blank Jr., a Vietnam veteran and a renowned expert on PTSD says in a video for The Washington Post. "People need to be able to talk about whatever they have to talk about to someone who is an experienced listener."

To supplement psychotherapy treatment for patients diagnosed with PTSD, sometimes doctors will prescribe medications like antidepressants as well as many other kinds of prescriptions that can help people along the road to recovery.

"I've been told by doctors that time will tell," Dana says. "Medication does only so much. Each individual has a different reaction to what traumas they suffer."

When asked if she had any advice for women going through a high conflict divorce, Dana offered this:

"Know when to give up the fight. I expected the legal system to protect me, to make sure my ex was punished when he defied court orders. I was proven wrong over and over again. My ex husband left and took 87% of his income, leaving me to raise two children on my own. I worried about feeding them, clothing them and housing them. I worried about their emotional welfare and I worked.

At times I worked two jobs to make ends meet. My children and I were trying to live our lives, struggling to get by and at the same time my ex was reaching in from a distance to make it just that much harder. You can't look to the legal system to protect you and the only way to win over someone who wants you to suffer is to give up the fight. Let it go, your health is more important.

Work constructively with your former partner on parenting issues One of the biggest things that damages children in a family is witnessing or suffering the effects of ongoing conflict between their parents. (Some children actually do better after parental separation if the new arrangement leads to less conflict and a more harmonious family environment.) For this reason, it is crucial that you work hard to develop a constructive relationship with your children's other parent. This is the single biggest factor that will help your children cope.
The more you can agree living and contact arrangements amicably and focus on your children's interests, the better it will be for them. A good way to do this is to develop a businesslike relationship with your former spouse; your aim is to move on from past hurts and to work constructively together as co-parents.
3 Help your children cope with divided loyalty It is very common for children to experience a divided loyalty between their parents. Make sure to give your children a balanced, fair and age-appropriate account of the separation

and how it happened, and reassure them that both their parents still love them. Ideally, this message should be given by both parents, together or separately, and repeated many times.

Speak positively about your ex-partner in front of the children, or, if you feel this is not honest, make it clear that your negative feelings are your own and allow your children to feel differently. Don't communicate through your kids or use them as a go-between. If you need to discuss something with their other parent, do so directly.

4 Listen to your children and focus on their best interests and needs Children cope differently with their parents' separation, depending on their age and personality. Listen carefully to your children individually to understand what support they need. Even children who appear to be coping fine need special understanding. A good idea is make sure you have one-to-one time with your kids. Periodically raise the topic of the separation and ask them what they think and feel about it, how they are coping. As they get older they will have further questions and thoughts. Work hard at keeping the lines of communication open.

5 Minimise the moves and changes in your child's life after separation Sometimes the major losses in children's lives are not directly due to the separation itself. Often they are related to the other changes the children experience, such as moving house, leaving a school, losing friends because of a move, or not seeing grandparents as often. While parents often feel they need a fresh start after separation, research seems to suggest that children need the opposite.

Try to maintain as many of the good things in your children's life as you can. This might mean making a special effort to ensure they keep in contact with grandparents or relatives from the other side of the family, or arranging things so that they can stay in the same school and see the same friends.

Dr John Sharry answers parenting questions in the *Irish Times* Health + Family supplement each Tuesday; he is also codeveloper of the Parents Plus: Parenting When Separated course (parentsplus.ie/ separation) and author of the new book *Parenting When Separated* (Veritas)

When you separate from your partner, you'll need to work out things like:

- where your children will live and how often they'll see the parent they don't live with
- where you're going to live

- how to divide up any money or belongings you share
- whether you'll be able to afford to pay the bills once you're living separately

If you're in the UK as a dependant on your partner's visa, you'll also need to check if you can stay - check if you can stay in the UK on a visa after a divorce.

Don't feel pressured into a decision that's not right for you. You'll have a better chance of reaching an agreement if you wait until you're ready to talk.

You need to have been married for at least 1 year before you can get divorced or dissolve your civil partnership, so there's usually time to work things out.

You'll usually need to talk to a solicitor at some point during your separation. To help keep your legal bills down, you should:

- try to agree as much as you can with your ex-partner before you go to a solicitor
- read as much as you can about separation - you could look online or go to the library
- find out if any solicitors near you offer free advice - this normally won't be more than 30 minutes, but it could still help
- ask your solicitor if they'll work for a fixed fee - this way, you'll always know exactly how much you'll have to pay

My marriage ended about four years ago. I won't tell you the reasons why, because every marriage that ends has its own reasons and they are all painful and sad. However, because of economic reasons, my ex and I were forced into what most would deem an intolerable situation: being separated but not being able to separate.

Our marriage was finished but we could not afford to spilt up with a mortgage, two kids and our own small business to support. So, I moved into the spare room as we both tried desperately to keep ourselves sane and functioning. Having two bathrooms helped.

The first couple of years were tough – panic attacks, fear, loathing (myself, him, the situation, the world) all featured constantly. I would wait embarrassingly at the school gates, hoping no one would notice me so I wouldn't have to smile and pretend. But secretly I was screaming for someone to help me. I didn't know how to ask and I was too afraid of judgment. Except for a few very close friends, no one knew. The shame of failure is a most powerful force.

In the past few years I have had to ask myself many times why this is? Why is the shame so heavy? Why, when I talk about my marriage ending, do people glaze over? Or, more often, become instantly distant? They back away suddenly to an errand they had forgotten needed their urgent attention. Or worse, they get preachy or angry at me, as if I am some kind of leper who still has the audacity to think they can continue to be part of society. I do not have an infectious condition.

Slowly, I've managed to let go of my own anger, disappointment and hurt and come to realise that these reactions are because there is one hugely popular narrative for the breakdown of marriage and it's not one of understanding. This bitter divorce storyline has become the standard for all of us because it is perfect at providing high-octane drama for TV, film and books.

I have heard myself talking, wishing for me to please shut up as I got entangled in the drama of it all

The basic narrative is this – a marriage breaks down, both parties hate each other. They fight and bicker and look for any opportunity to stab one another in the back or get one-ups on the other. They go to court for a long drawn-out battle where the only winners are the lawyers. The kids get screwed up because of the whole process. Finally the exes go their separate ways but neither one ever, ever forgives or forgets the betrayal or hurt of the other.

Empathy

This story is okay if you have some distance from it but you certainly don't want it coming around for a cup of tea and crying on your shoulder asking for empathy. I understand that it's scary and uncomfortable. I have heard myself talking, wishing for me to please shut up as I got entangled in the drama of it all and knowing I am selling something that shouldn't even be for sale.

But now I have a different story.

It started out with flailing for solutions. When I had the strength, I would frantically crunch numbers and look at job sites hoping something would add up to an escape route. Nothing ever did and perhaps that was because most of my energy was taken up with pretending everything was okay while being a working partner in the business and raising two kids. I zombie-walked through days, then paced my room all night. There were some days when I actually hid in a cupboard.

Then, one day in a shopping centre, I ran into another woman who was going through a break-up. As I listened to her pain and anger, I felt myself sinking into a hole of helplessness. Her anger was palpable and understandable and my heart ached for her too. But listening to her struggles, I realised that I could make a decision. I could decide how I was going to be. I could decide who I was going to be. And with that one realisation everything changed.

It was extremely hard at first. Like everyone, I wanted vindication and validation

From that point on, I tried to base all my other decisions from this basic premise – who did I want to be?

It was extremely hard at first. Like everyone, I wanted vindication and validation but I was never going to get what I wanted – that's why the marriage had ended in the first place. I recognised that my power was in who I decided to be, not proving who was right or wrong. After years of feeling helpless and trapped, I had a sense of power back and I began to heal. I could decide who I wanted to be – not for the good of anyone else but me. I could make my life better no matter the circumstances.

All the things that hurt me or made me angry about the marriage were no longer relevant because we (yes, he and I) had decided to not be married. I had to change my expectations of him and he of me. I stopped apologising for myself, started to see who I was and started to let go of my old idea of who he was or should be.

I don't know when, but at some point in year three, we both decided that we were to no longer discuss the past. We had a new relationship now where the issues of being husband and wife were no longer relevant. We were now a partnership raising two children and keeping a business afloat.

But I can't tell you much about his journey because we also decided that certain things were none of our business any more. This can be hugely liberating.

I, of course, must acknowledge that my ex had his own healing to do and he worked hard at becoming a great dad and rebuilding our relationship into something new.

But I can't tell you much about his journey because we also decided that certain things were none of our business any more. This can be hugely liberating.

Now I can very proudly say that we are friends.

All four of us still live in the same house and neither he nor I see any reason to change this even if we could. I have no desire for our children to see less of their father. For us, ironically, it has now become the easier option to stay. Honestly, I do not know if we would have reached this point if we had not been forced into this situation but man, am I glad now that we were.

Weird

People, of course find it weird and I can see most can't get their head around it. "Surely you will get back together," or "It's just like being married then except you don't sleep together," they say. But it's not.

It is so far from that.

But it is hard to explain. We are not a couple but we are not room-mates. We are also not just friends because we have two kids together and a history. The simplest way I can put it is, it's a new mindset; it's a new kind of family.

I just wanted to put it out there that the story of a marriage separation can be known

It's our family.

There are still plenty of hiccups and arguments and working out stuff but we are both sure that this is the best solution, for us . . . at this moment.

And that is the best anyone can wish for no matter what their circumstances.

Of friends, let me say this. Mine are the best. No, really, the best. Those special few who patiently held my hand or kicked my arse . . . they are the best people I know and I will never be able to repay such kindness.

I just wanted to put it out there that the story of a marriage separation can be different. They are never easy, they are never not sad but they can help you develop into something new. A new type of friendship. It is not the most exciting story, but I can tell you everyone comes out okay in the end.

By societal standards, my divorce was as easy as they come. But a lot of work went into having a healthy divorce.

I am grateful every day that my kids' father and I did everything we could to understand why we had come together and why we needed to come apart. We both loved being parents to our children, so we wanted to remain a family in every way possible while living in two homes.

Parents provide the floor under their children's feet and divorce often pulls that floor out from underneath them — it can leave a child feeling rootless and terrified. I know those feelings well from my own childhood: from the age of four, my mother wasn't able to care for us. I grew up on very shaky ground, moving to new homes and cities, with a father who was divorced three times by the end of my teens.

When it came to my own divorce, I wanted a different experience. A child's universe does not need to be decimated just because the two adults in charge of them are changing the form of their relationship.

My ex-husband was equally committed to keeping the foundation intact under our children's feet. Despite our personal views about our relationship and why it was ending, we put our children first. We were ending our marriage, not ending our family.

Our formula for a healthy divorce required certain steps ... Below are eight tips for all couples ending their marriage who *don't* wish to end their family:

1. Really understand your marriage (and divorce) before you pull the trigger.

It's essential to understand your marriage with your partner — whether in couple's therapy or elsewhere. Try getting a sense of perspective by talking to others about their experiences (friends or through social media platforms like Splitsville). From there, you'll be better able to dig deep into the impact of divorce *before* moving out.

This process will help you figure out how best to communicate the emotional message to your kids, in addition to the seismic logistical shifts.

2. Explore and try out alternative ways of structuring your new family system before making any final decisions.

My ex-husband and I tried a four-month period of what we called "nesting" to discover what a separation really felt like before making a final decision to divorce. Of course, this will help you and your partner; but it will also make the shift more gradual for your children.

3. Stay as close as possible to each other while maintaining appropriate boundaries.

My ex-husband and I kept our homes four blocks from each other as another way to make the change more gradual. We did this to avoid creating a feeling of real "distance" to our children.

4. Put effort into the details to create cozy environments for everyone.

We were committed to ensuring that both homes were properly set up and comfortable for the kids. This included furniture, toys, bedding and blankets they liked to sleep with at night and so on.

5. Create and maintain clear, consistent boundaries.

While my ex-husband and I chose to live close by to one another, we also created and agreed upon a very clear and consistent parenting schedule. Boundaries are important to keep consistency — both for us as parents, and for our children. To this day, we are painstakingly vigilant about maintaining a consistent rhythm in our children's lives so there is never the question of "*Who's house am I staying at tonight?*"

6. Transcend yourself for the bigger picture (well, at least for a few days a year).

We sacrifice individually-desired vacation plans for the sake of our children. How? We have tried one vacation rental in August and split the time staying there. This allows us to have necessary separation from one another, while allowing our kids stability: they stay there the whole month, and we rotate.

7. Share one credit card for all expenses to help with transparency and accountability.

We share one credit card for all kid-related expenses — but with a limit on what one can spend without running it past the other.

Divorced couples often argue about expenses and create more work for themselves with receipts, cancelled checks and bank statements. I actually find it baffling why more co-parents don't do this: it's the

While you might have been thrilled to have the opportunity to be a stay-at-home mom with your kids, now that your marriage has turned sour you're finding that leaving will be very challenging. While there is no doubt that hard times lie ahead, if you're determined, you can make a workable plan to exit your unhappy union. It'll require time and plenty of hard work, and you'll also have to step outside your comfort zone. If you're convinced that continuing to stay married will equal a lifetime of misery, however, this will be a small sacrifice.

Make a plan. While walking out the door today will likely leave you in dire economic straits, doing so a few months from now after you've had a chance to save some money is entirely feasible. Figure out how much money you will need to leave by researching the costs of local apartments, child care and other expenses you'll incur.

Get a job. If it's been a while since you've worked, ask a friend to help you put together a current resume. Visit your state employment agency to find out what is available for a person with your skill set. Persist in looking for employment, even if it appears nothing is available. Wait tables or clean houses while you look for the position you want, according to tips on "Dr. Phil" McGraw's website. Enjoy the process, which may serve to distract you from your distressing marriage.

Make child care arrangements. If you have your children in a day care facility that you trust, leaving your marriage will be much easier. Child care can be quite expensive. Consider choosing a facility that will accept any child care subsidies that are available for low-income people in your state. For example, the state of Texas has a Child Care Management Services program that can help you pay for day care. While you may not qualify while you are still living with your husband, you can apply for assistance once you are paying your expenses on your own.

Gather a support system. Look for people who might be interested in sharing housing so you can save on expenses. Make a friend with whom you can trade child care favors should you need to work overtime and require someone to pick up your kids from school or day care. To avoid being perceived as needy, offer as much as you give.

Save your money diligently. Pass up opportunities to shop clothing sales and put every last penny that you don't need for bills into a savings account that is in your name. If your husband is controlling or abusive, don't let him know you are saving money in order to leave him.

Find a new home and file for divorce. If money is tight, which it almost certainly will be, seek legal assistance from a nonprofit organization designed to assist people with low incomes. If necessary, at this point you can also seek state assistance to help you pay for groceries and housing until you get on your feet.

Parents have an **equal** legal right to custody of their child when their relationship ends. No parent has a greater legal right to custody over another parent, even if they did most of the child care or were abused by another parent. Only a court order or agreement changes this equal right.

If you leave your partner and take your child with you, your partner might say that you ignored their equal right to custody. Your partner might even say that you abducted the child.

The family court might order that your child be returned to your partner's care if it thinks that is in the best interests of the child. However, this does not mean you must leave your child behind when you leave your partner.

You should talk to a lawyer before you leave your partner. Your lawyer can help you make parenting plans with your partner before you leave, if it is safe. These can be short-term plans that say where the child lives and when they see each parent.

If you don't make these plans with your partner before you leave and take your child with you, you or your lawyer can write a letter to your partner. The letter should say that you want to talk about custody and access issues.

If it is **safe**, tell your partner how to contact you. Or, tell them that you will contact them within a day or two.

If it is **not safe**, leave a message for your partner once you are in a safe place. Take steps so that they cannot easily find you.

You should include ways to keep you safe when making custody and access plans.

Welcome! To bring you the best content on our sites and applications, Meredith partners with third party advertisers to serve digital ads, including personalized digital ads. Those advertisers use tracking technologies to collect information about your activity on our sites and applications and across the Internet and your other apps and devices.

You always have the choice to experience our sites without personalized advertising based on your web browsing activity by visiting the, the , and/or the , from each of your browsers or devices. To avoid personalized advertising based on your mobile app activity, you can You can find much more information about your privacy choices in our privacy policy. SEPSEPEven if you choose not to have your activity tracked by third parties for advertising services, you will still see non-personalized ads on our site.

By clicking continue below and using our sites or applications, you agree that we and our third party advertisers can:

Going through a separation or divorce can be very difficult, no matter the reason for it. It can turn your world upside down and make it hard to get through the work day and stay productive. But there are things you can do to get through this difficult adjustment.

Recognize that it's OK to have different feelings. It's normal to feel sad, angry, exhausted, frustrated and confused—and these feelings can be intense. You also may feel anxious about the future. Accept that reactions like these will lessen over time. Even if the marriage was unhealthy, venturing into the unknown is frightening.

Give yourself a break. Give yourself permission to feel and to function at a less than optimal level for a period of time. You may not be able to be quite as productive on the job or care for others in exactly the way you're accustomed to for a little while. No one is superman or superwoman; take time to heal, regroup and re-energize.

Don't go through this alone. Sharing your feelings with friends and family can help you get through this period. Consider joining a support group where you can talk to others in similar situations. Isolating yourself can raise your stress levels, reduce your concentration, and get in the way of your work, relationships and overall health. Don't be afraid to get outside help if you need it.

Take care of yourself emotionally and physically. Be good to yourself and to your body. Take time out to exercise, eat well and relax. Keep to your normal routines as much as possible. Try to avoid making major decisions or changes in life plans. Don't use alcohol, drugs or cigarettes as a way to cope; they only lead to more problems.

Avoid power struggles and arguments with your spouse or former spouse. If a discussion begins to turn into a fight, calmly suggest that you both try talking again later and either walk away or hang up the phone.

Take time to explore your interests. Reconnect with things you enjoy doing apart from your spouse. Have you always wanted to take up painting or play on an intramural softball team? Sign up for a class, invest time in your hobbies, volunteer, and take time to enjoy life and make new friends.

Think positively. Easier said than done, right? Things may not be the same, but finding new activities and friends, and moving forward with reasonable expectations will make this transition easier. Be flexible. If you have children, family traditions will still be important but some of them may need to be adjusted. Help create new family activities.

Life will get back to normal, although "normal" may be different from what you had originally hoped.

Tips for talking to kids …

If you have children, here's a short list of tips that can help your young children and teens cope.

Reassure and listen. Make sure your kids know that your divorce is not their fault. Listen to and ease their concerns, and be compassionate but direct in your responses.

Maintain stability and routines. Try to keep your kids' daily and weekly routines as familiar and stable as possible.

Offer consistent discipline. Now that your kids may share time with both parents separately, make sure to agree in advance on bedtimes, curfews and other everyday decisions, as well as any punishments.

Let your children know they can rely on you. Make and keep realistic promises. And don't overly confide in them about your feelings about the divorce.

Don't involve your children in the conflict. Avoid arguing with or talking negatively about the other parent in front of your kids. Don't use them as spies or messengers, or make them take sides

In any given year, only 60% of people with a mental illness get mental health care. As a result, family members and caregivers often play a large role in helping and supporting them.

Millions of people have experienced the thoughts and questions you might be having now. You may be trying to help a family member who doesn't have access to care or doesn't want help. Or you may want to learn how to support and encourage someone who has been hospitalized or experienced a similar mental health crisis. Take a look at this infographic we developed with our friends at HealthCentral for some ideas on how to support a loved one

The Biter truth of Biter Devoice and child custody struggling

forgive your ex even for most inexcusable behaviour ridiculing you for minor flaws and infractions

Parental alienation is a problem that most often arises when parents engage in bitter and extended child custody struggling. At times intense feelings of anger and mistrust are common when parents are struggling to transition from marriage wave of emotions surrounding divorce into a co-parenting relationship. Most often some parents experience less anger and anxiety over such times rather they make efforts to co-parent in a way that it will be healthier and more productive for the children.

The Parental alienation occurs when a child is influenced by other parent often called the *alienator* as to completely reject the other parent often known as the *target one*. In most severe cases, alienation results in the other child completely rejection of the target parent. Usually, the reasons for the rejection are unfounded or unjustified, according to parental educator and author

Owning to the intensity of emotions that will erupt during the lengthy process of separation and divorce, so many parents will experience strain and frustration within the parent's relationship to the said child. This will allow some parents engage in harmful and destructive behaviours that eventually lead to the natural consequence of the child rejecting the said parent from other parent. For better explanation, true parental alienation takes place when one parent intentionally influences the other child to behaviour negatively to the other parent in a horrible way. Although negative manner but does not mean there had being evidence of abusive, destructive or harmful parenting behaviours. One can only admit if the five common signs that a child is being affected by true parental alienation.

These are; the child's views towards the alienating parent to show as the good and honest parent which does not expresses only negative feelings toward the target parent but also ridicule him as bad parent. This ridiculing thinking will consistently reinforced by the alienating parent until the child expresses hatred, contempt and fear regarding the target parent without not showing any guilt or remorse to worsen the situation. The child often denies being coached or influenced by one parent. Accusations and opinions of the alienating parent do insist that the child have to formulate ideas about the target parent on their own.

Another negativity that exists is the tension targeted parent is also extending to the extended family and therefore the child beginning to show signs of disobedience in their communication to the opposite parents. The direct and collateral damages may also result from parental alienation to long-lasting effects that are enormously destructive and destabilizing to both the children together with the parents involved.

Alienation affection and damages the child's sense of self and her ability to form lasting opinion, in relationships to their friends and family. The loss of connection of the alienated parent also damages the child's psychological thinking and understanding when it comes to her views, since she will now lack one parent as a role model without being able to benefit from that loss parent.

Parental alienation has such destructive long-term consequences for both parents and children, this extremely concerning that more is not being done by professionals to help the situation when early stage alienation happen to be taking place and take strategic actions to turn things around before it reaches critical and damaging stage. One unfortunate thing about child alienating is that, many courts and professionals who deal with cases are not trained to handle high-conflict divorce cases therefore they're unable to detect alienation at early stages where professional intervention could have the greatest impact of preventing the situation. Alienation is often hard to define or legally prove and many target parents trying to prove parental alienation in court which prove quite challenging, expensive and time-consuming.

Even if these parents are willing to do so, many of such court systems are not equipped to deal with such high-conflict parenting situations that need intensive intervention. In many occasion the courts systems are reluctant to deal with such cases or not even unable to effectively intervene in a consistently effective manner, for these parents are often find out that the family law attorneys cannot either minimize the situation and are reluctant to pursue the issues in court.

Many complicating cases cannot be followed up further, whence some parents refuse to participate in parent-child therapy and respond to guidance from a therapist and parenting coordinators unless it is ordered by the court and carefully monitored and evaluated on an on-going basis. In certain cases, the alienating parents usually use well-experienced litigation as a means to control the target parent, but many target parents are exhausted by cases of litigation and may fear that more legal intervention will only worsen the situation.

Parents seeking professional intervention truly understand the underlying dynamics of the problem before trying hard not to take the child's rejection personally but stay committed to positive co-parenting attitude. This also sometime advises parents to not give up hope despite the complexity of the situation. Because the journey to repair your relationship with your child involve can be long and often requires an enormous amount of patience and persistence. Child relationships sometimes it may take years before you will see the results of your choices and effort. Always think positive and never ever make the mistake of thinking you can do everything when it comes to the matter of your children's behaviour towards you. You can be more experience of these signs but it can turn to a strategy in which you can't help it any longer. Divorce Management Coach provides at Moving Forward in many occasions yet Divorce provides guidance to women and men as they learn how to manage the chaos that comes after the divorce. Combination of experiences such as a Family Law Paralegal which provides coaching and Training to clients with the resources, skills and strategies they need to save time, money and avoid headaches as they navigate through divorce. There are programs to learn about what harms children of divorce the most endure. Many affordable divorce coaching program, and Divorce seminars also includes a track devoted to parenting after divorce.

These are sufficient information on which to form an opinion. The way of your parenting time or contact between parenting circumstances of your divorce and your child's character could all play into evil's den. If the child tries to stay with you mean she will be going to miss some play dates with her friends and may wish she didn't have come to you. At the same time not want to tell you that because she doesn't want to hurt your feelings. He may not next time, want to come until she's settled down and happy and then have the conversation with you by reassuring her that she can be honest with you, that you're concerned about her well-being. Ask open questions and be sure not to paraphrase them to make her feel she has to choose or speak against the other parent. There is one tiny voice that silenced anyone who still had doubts that parental alienation is real and one of the most insidious forms of child abuse.

A boy openly made up his mind and lied about his father concerning his step-mother and threw himself widely opened to criticism some years back when the father was away working for the betterment him and his sideling. But his case was brought up at his father's divorce case where they were to meet for settlement by his devastated mother who has endured a 12-year court battle with her ex-husband to try to win back the heart and mind of their son.

Gimah has been one tiny soldier in the growing army of bitter children who are becoming collateral damage in bitter battles between ex-spouses that are overwhelming in Africa divorce courts, the first of its kind Symposium for Parental Alienation Syndrome (PAS) heard during these battles in Ghana.

Over 11 years had four different lawyers trying to convince the courts of a son who lived less than 20 hours flight from the father who needed to see the mother who loved and raised him which was told to the conference.

It is sometime a believed that no parent would wound their child for their own selfish gain. But people still believe that losing your parent is not all that big a deal because you can lose your parents when they get old or when they get sick or even get car accidents and die. But alienated parents aren't dead but are alive which the children know it.

According to Gimah's father it was her ex-girlfriend who began a fears campaign to solely seal the custody of their then 14-year old son and cut off all communication links to the father by his mother both physically and psychologically, shortly after the couple separated in 2001.

For PAS children generally there are no tangible signs of maltreatment by both sides but it is kidnapping of the mind which normally term as A Heart-breaking Story of Parental Alienation Syndrome.

Parental Alienation Syndrome has everything to do with who has custody of the said child. It's an idling calculated opportunity that are always argued against each parent in a battle to gain what have been produce by the two people whether is a syndrome or a mental health disorder or abuse just ties everyone up in knots while real children and real families suffer this strategy. What is usually seen as child's fundamental right to be loved by both his and her parents is rather destroyed by such wicked and cruelty by both parents just by lack of understanding.

The effects are long-lasting as far as both parents do not subside in their alienation ventures and are always doing more just to win the argument.

Adults who were alienated when they were children revealed that lifelong battles with low self-esteem, alcoholism and drug abuse, as well as high bad behaviour and fail in academic ventures

Parental alienation can to be known as malicious mother Dilemma but it's become opportunity form of emotional abuse of children over the last two decades, owning to a new study of some the growing trend cases in recent history of our world.

In 2001 when our struggle of child custody started it was seen among high-conflict divorce cases examined which has crippled families. Generally men turned their kids against their mothers, while so many of the cases involved women alienating the kids against their fathers.

African family courts have decided to deal contentiously with divorces cases by awarding sole custody to one parent, believing that joint custody is simply unworkable among most African partners who are at war.

Most divorce experts including mental health professionals and child advocacy workers, some of them take the fight to conferences, have long argued that this approach encourages parental alienation by treating the children as prizes to be won or lost in bitter battle.

The only results confirmed in the usual divorce laws needed to be amended to make equal shared parenting a norm in all divorce cases, except strange circumstances such as domestic violence, mental health or other issues that will make the other parent clearly unfit.

In a case where the alienated parents is non-custodial fathers to engage those fathers is a significant challenge which sometimes one can be seen as the opposite individual who is not fit by lack of emanating from two sources the characteristics of men and fathers themselves. Traditional Patterns of gender-equality role can also direct men toward self-sufficiency and control independent problem-solving and emotional restraint to have largely worked against fathers being unable to acknowledge their short comings and ask for help. For the fear of self-disclosure and a feeling of disloyalty to their family to expose these families' problems is common fear of losing control over their life and the need to present an image of control. In the form of exterior calm, strength, and rationality, despite considerable inner turmoil which usually characterizes many fathers they try to maintain their position. Professional service providers also do not always consider such psychological obstacles to therapy and thus do not address fathers' unique needs. The research on divorced fathers shows clearly about their most pressing need of their continued meaningfully involvement with their children, as active parents. The lack of recognition of this primary need is the main reason why most professional's lack of success in engaging alienated fathers.

Pertaining to the key to engaging alienated parents is to validate their parental identity, and combine advocacy efforts with counselling to focus on enhancing their role as active and responsible father. Professionals who for recently have been notably seen dangers of absentee father in the politics of reform with respect to the issue of legal child custody which the society are desperately indeed of as allies in policy reform efforts. The greatest important role of human service professionals should be supporting alienated parents through such advocacy and activisms, challenging the custodial and non-custodial residential parent duties are to advancing the cause of co-parenting.

An active program to educate an individual on this subject is essential as alienated parents report lack this effective support services and therefore remain a highly vulnerable population. Professional service providers need to be persistent and proactive and take time to build and sustain engagement in the context of these parents' feelings of isolation, helplessness, and their tendency to wait until there is a crisis before accessing support. Parents who were highly involved with are attached to their children and suddenly find themselves forcefully removed from their children's lives experience profound wontedness. Those parents who are experiencing of being removed from loving parent life of one's child by a sole custody order strikes the heart of many individual fathers. These sees suicide rates reports at epidemic proportions among such parents fathers in particular, who always struggling to maintain a parenting relationship with their children legal abuse as a key factor in these cases. Being vigilant regarding symptoms of post-traumatic stress and suicidal ideation among non-custodial and alienated fathers and mothers is an essential role for professional service providers. A struggling-based approach is by the way of recognizing alienated parent's aspirations to their children's wellbeing especially to impart experience, knowledge and skills that they can contribute to this welfare of the child while addressing the alienation problems.

There are many areas of concern for social workers working with divorced or separated couples with children who are facing the problems of parental alienation. Their efforts on these parents are to turn a child who may be against the other parent, and parental alienation syndrome, or a child's unwarranted rejection of one parent in response to the attitudes and actions of the other parent. Social workers will encounter these problems in a number of ways, such as family service agencies, schools, and family court, as well as private practice working with high-conflict divorcing couples. These parents who believe that the other parent has or will turn the children against them as alienated children will refuse to see such a parent, adults who are still alienated from a parent or elders who have lost their children battle to parental alienation.

Some social workers may be unaware of the name Parental Alienation Syndrome for this particular problem yet they have probably dealt with it over the course of their careers. For example individual clients may enter individual counselling therapy to solve the problem of depression, or relationship problems and later reveal that they have been cut off from one parent by another parent. These clients may be unaware of the meaning of the lost relationship and may even minimize its effect on their development, and current mental health concerns.

Children academic record in school or in the society may prompt the social workers casually reveal that they have no contact with a hated parent. When questioned about the absent parent, these children may vehemently denounce the parent as bad and rubbish. The parents of such a child may be manoeuvring behind the scenes to exclude the other parent from the child's school life by misrepresenting that parent's intentions to school staff, withholding information from that parent to create the appearance of a lack of interest, and removing contact information from school records. Another scenario the represented clients who enter therapy counselling is consumed with fear that the other parent is turning the children against them. Such parents will be desperate for advice and guidance about how to cope with the provocation of the other parent. These parents live with anxiety, depression, and helplessness, as well as feelings of victimization by the other parents. The children and the legal systems deals with legal and mental health issues that is not always responsive to the needs of targeted parents.

In such cases social workers may formulate ways that will defined the other one parent and engineer the child's rejection of the other parent. But unless the social worker is familiar with parental alienation as an act of parental alienation syndrome, he or she may be missing useful information for understanding how one parent is able to poison a child's relationship with the other parent in the absence of just cause.

Child Custody struggle is known as Parental alienation and it is a strategy that a parent uses to undermine and to foster a child's rejection of the other parent. Parental alienation syndrome in not new in the developed world, It develops in children who come to hate, fear, and reject the targeted parent as someone unworthy of having caring heart to coined the other children to hate the other parent known as Parental alienation syndrome as already described.

How a mother will campaign against her Divorce husband to gain access to her children.
Children are engulfing with hatred of the targeted parent that leads to alienating. They do not remember any positive past experiences with such father only to reject all contact and communication to satisfy the alienator. Men who once loved and valued his children overnight has become hated and feared.

If you ask the alienated children about the reasons for their intense hostility toward the targeted parent they cannot offer any better explanations to the magnitude that typically to the rejection that parent. Some of these children may complain about the parent's eating habits, food preparation or their caring attitude some also make wild accusations that turns out possibly be true. These affected alienated children exhibit a lack of affection of their alienated parent and therefore demonstrating an automatic hatred and dislike to support their action. The alienator parent is perceived as perfect while the father is also seen as useless in his effort to win the once loved child like him again. If an alienated child is asked to identify any bad thing the alienated father has done that justify negative aspect of the alienating parent probably draw a negative utterances. These show the fact that most children have mixed feelings about even the best parents they may have.

There are many different ways to confirm that one has been manipulated by a parent to unnecessarily reject the other parent and what region catalysts the other parent to represents both good and bad news of the other. We have good news that many ways families adapted to resolve from alienation to realization. But there is no magic to reach this process only if one is willing to sort peace through this channel. Even though some affected parents have their own way of doing it is a matter of time before one will gain experience. Others use the alienating parent as an example being alienated by someone turning on them and, for others; it is becoming a parent being the target of parental alienating from their own children.

There are a few cases that are sore, resulting from the either the father will take a horrible discussion that may end the lives of the family together or may kill himself from such useless situation. Sometimes things slowly chip itself away from of a long-held belief system, which awaken a different truth and a more authentic. Such gained self-respect connection to reality may be grateful to know the truth. This self-acknowledgement that turns this truth is hard be won and quite painful. Once the parents are aware of the parental alienation, they had to come to terms with this painful truth that the alienating parent did not have their best interest at heart, these children they have, probably behaved very differently toward someone like them who did not deserve such treatment, and that they missed out on a relationship that may have real value and benefit to their life.

It May be probably surprising, that adult children who have parental alienation syndrome believed that the experience will have negative long-term consequences on their life but are unable to find solution to such problem. Many says they're suffering from depression and therefore turn to drugs and alcohol to quench their pain, but failed relationships and multiple divorces most sadly, becoming alienated from their own children later in life. These are the ways, the intergenerational cycle of parental alienation syndrome as perpetuated.

These are some Alienation Tactics.

Some of the adult children with parental alienation syndrome devise a wild range of alienating strategies, including constant bad behaviour against of the targeted parent, chronic interference with visitation, communication, and emotional manipulation to choose one parent over the other. There had been more than 1,300 specific actions to describe these. There had been a considerable attempts complete overlap in the strategies identified by the targeted parents with those described by adult children.

What are the problems working with Targeted Parents

Professionals workers counselling parents who are facing parental alienation who need support, education, and guidance suffer allot. Such worker's primary role is to help their client about parental alienating what primary behaviours that a child will display against the other parent and parental alienation syndrome what that behavioural manifestations of an alienated child so the parent can determine the facts about the problem. These clients must be encouraged to look at themselves and their relationship with their children prior to blaming the other parent for their difficulties.

The conclusions will be that parental alienation may work against the targeted parent and therefore should be taught a series of responses to prevent parental alienation. This can allow the targeted parent to maintain the highest behaviour not becoming overly passive or reactive. The greatest possible thing such parents need is daily validation and support in dealing with the pain and suffering associated with parental alienation.

Another way is working With Alienated Children

Professional Social workers who volunteer help children currently who are alienated must be self-reflective in other words an example to follow and be aware so that they do not collide with the child against the targeted parent. A second concern is to avoid becoming intimidated or manipulated by the alienating parent also against their target. The child should learn to develop critical thinking skills in order to help him or her ability to resist the pressure to choose to move away from this behaviour. The affected child's attitude to targeted parent and their relationship to that parent must be validated for the child to advice the child of his or her next step. Such worker can be a role model who values and respects the targeted parent in order to counter the behaviour message that this parent should discard, private practitioners family service agencies or school settings, social workers who are working with clients affected should be able to help the parental alienation victims. Some of these individuals may even be unaware of the source of such pain and suffering or uninformed about the name and nature of this phenomenon. Familiarity on the worker is the first step to provide the client with better information, guidance, and hope when dealing with this complicated and painful issue like this. Nothing stirs up controversy more than the controversy generated when parents are at war over the custody of a child.

Controversies are an issue where evidence on both sides can make a compelling case. It may never be polarized whether black and white, but when people have their emotions flare up on an issue it can quickly turn into two polar opposites.

Fairness takes over reasoning, incomplete facts become evidence, and court schedules become complicated with repeated visits to a judge to try to bring sanity to whoever is unlikely to ever be insane. One thing to beware of is social movements who may be promoting one side over another in their feeble justice. The court maintains pass laws to bring order to chaos but when Gender wars are fuelled lives are destroyed.

How I became exposure to custody wars stems from Social parental show from United Kingdom where Parent fight bitterly over their kids every day. Many of these parents in such gathering show classes were litigating over child custody. In such motion shows most wanted to settle the case, but none of them would like to give access of the child to the other which seemed to be the only alternative open to them for settlement.

It was quiet disturbing to see that in such many cases, the child will behave outrageously, to the point of cursing their parents, even kick, spit on them and calls them stupid, a horrible thing that usually happens. All people will be sitting unconcern because no one can help them out of such terrible situation unless they come to their senses of the damage being cause to their child. What can you or one do when the children are caught up in such a fight and starts taking sides I came to realize that at such a level of conflict in custody disputes the fallout is from sweeping societal changes around in our society?

When can these changes help to shape the society?

Since the end of the 1970's, women have taken more active role in going to work and going back to college to pursue careers as never before. This shift has bought many changes to our society and became more women getting involved in the day-to-day carrier building more than what it was truly in previous generations. The complications are when parental roles began to fall apart, than the *tender years* where the parental doctrine was still in place. As our religious doctrine still convict us that by virtue of the fact that a women is the keeper of the home as the mother of our kids. Couples were the mother of our children that they must be the superior parents. In the early 1970's several coutries obey the no fault divorce laws, where anyone who wanted out of a marriage was free to leave. Some have called it the no guilt laws. There was a proliferation of divorce that was historically unprecedented.

After a family breakup, many fathers wanted to continue to be involved with the care of their children. Suddenly, they found that they had no legal right to have custody of their children unless the mother agreed to it.

Due to the lobbying efforts of James Cook, founder of the Joint Custody Association, who was caught up in this problem himself, this made California legislature s passed the first joint custody laws.

Joint custody was widely seen as a better way of handling this problem by evolving both parents to share child custody equally. It was then perceived that would lead to fewer fights over the custody of children because it was more equal opportunity for both parents. These followed by other states in United State also passed joint custody laws that allow both parents to enjoy their children presence every day equally. These laws helped to bring peace as is seen as level the playing field for fathers.

The most mothers and fathers welcomed joint custody as fair. Others even don't want to see the children's father come in contact with them. There was backlash since child custody become highly sensitive issue with the ramping up of high-level disputes ever since the changes in our society. In most countries the tender years of the child's years is presumed as the mother knows best has been replaced with the best interests for the child as joint custody which is seen as the best for both parents.

In the beginning of 1980's, the Law began to increasingly ignore gender in determining child custody. This removed the automatic full custody rights to the mother and these lead to having less time with their children. Instead the Law looked first at how the custody could be shared but if that is seen as impossible the judicial officers attempted to determine which parent was more interested and better able to attend to the best interest of the child.

This Lead the Fathers perceived that they were at risk of disadvantage because of bias toward the mother having permanent custody rights. Because of this more fathers than never showing up at parenting classes to make sure that their skills also can make a difference. This made the Authorises take up the issues and paid attention to its contents.

Most parents were able to share custody of their children, and they worked out childcare issues in an amicable.

A large number of women were even relieved to have fathers share in the childcare, which enabled them to pursue their personal life goals in their educational career.

However, when the atmosphere became unfriendly to resolve child custody the fathers found themselves that they have greater opportunity to gain joint or primary custodial status by going to court. The issue got even higher when the legal system was used to resolve these difficult problems evenly. In most hard cases, the alienation of a child's affection against a targeted parent became a bizarre escalation of the intensity of more conflict.

Who discovered Parental Alienation Syndrome (PAS)?

With growing child-custody cases forensic psychiatrist Dr. Richard A. Gardner first identified Parental Alienation Syndrome in the 1980's. He noticed that the issue need to be addressed as dramatic increase in the frequency of child custody disorder rarely as observed before the programming of brainwashing of a child by one parent to alienate the other parent.

However, the disorder wasn't just brainwashing or programming by a parent. It was a serious founded issue that Dr. Gardner calls it self-created contributions by the child in support of the alienating parent's campaign of denigration against the targeted parent. He called this disorder Parental Alienation Syndrome (PAS), a new term that includes the contribution to the problem made by both the parent and the child. He defines it as follows;

1. The Parental Alienation Syndrome is a disorder that arises primarily in the context of child-custody disputes.

2. Its primary manifestation is the child's campaign of denigration against a parent, a campaign that has no justification.

3. It results from the combination of brainwashing of a parent's indoctrinations and the child's own contributions to the vilification of the targeted parent. This extract is from: Gardner, R.A. (1998). The Parental Alienation Syndrome, Second Edition, Cresskill, NJ: Creative Therapeutics, Inc.

These are the child's contribution to the part in PAS

Gardner notes that the PAS is more than brainwashing or programming, because the child has to actually participate in the denigrating of the alienated parent. This is done in primarily the following eight ways:

1. The child denigrates the alienated parent with abusive language and severe oppositional behaviour.
2. The child usually offers weak, absurd, or frivolous reasons for his or her anger.
3. The child will be sure of himself or herself and doesn't demonstrate i.e. love and hate for the alienated parent, only hate.
4. The child will come up with ideas of denigration. This phenomenon is where the child asserts that no one told him to do this.
5. The child supports professional feels that there should be a need to protect the alienating parent.
6. The child always does not demonstrate guilt over cruelty towards their alienated parent.
7. The child uses borrowed words scenarios to describe the situations or she could not have experienced.
8. The situation is sometimes spread to the friends and extended family of the alienated parent.

In severe cases of parent alienation the child is utterly brain- washed against the alienated parent. The alienator can truthfully say that the child doesn't want to spend any time with the other parent even though he or she has mighty secure court injunction. The alienator typically will say there isn't anything that I can do about it. I'm not telling him not to see you.

PAS is an escalation part of Parental Alienation which Dr. Douglas Darnall in his book Divorce Casualties: Protecting Your Children from Parental Alienation describes three categories of PA:

These are mild categories which he calls it's the naïve alienators. They are ignorant of damage they cause to the child and they need to be educated and change.

The moderate once are the active alienators. When they are triggered, they lose control of appropriate boundaries. They use their abusive languages and when they calm down, they don't want to admit that they were out of control.

The severe categories are the obsessed alienators or those who are involved in parental alienation syndrome. They operate from a delusional system where every cell of their body committed to destroying the other parent's relationship with the child. His latter case, he wrote that we don't have an effective protocol for treating obsessed alienators other than removing the child from their influence.

The important point in Parental Alienating Syndrome is that no true parental abuse and neglect on the part of the alienated parent. If it is true in each case, the child's animosity would be justified. In other way Parental Alienating Syndrome is not that the child still has a positive relationship with the parent, even though one parent is attempting to alienate the child from him or her.

According to most likely to initiate Parental Alienating Syndrome cases Gardner's statistics showed that the majority of PAS occurrences are initiated by mothers. Mothers have traditionally had primary custody of the children before the 20th century Law which favour both parents, but the mothers usually want to spend more time with their children.

In order to advert alienating of a child one parent needs to have considerable time with the child. However, in recent years increasing numbers of fathers have started instigating Parental Alienating Syndrome, since there are no strong Laws or legal sanctions for doing so.

There are a few cases where the fathers were seen as the alienators.

In one case, the father had no control over his obsession to trash the mother.

Numerous professionals told him, including the mother, that he could have shared custody if he would be willing to follow the rules. He didn't have the self-control to do this.

When he lost custody because of his aberrant behaviour, he became a celebrity in the father's rights movement and took his campaign into national circles. No one would know from hearing him speak about his situation that there was serious pathology going on (PAS) or how hard the professionals worked to stabilize it.

Moreover, in cultures where women traditionally have no tangible rights, alienation by the father can be severe.

I've met divorcing women who had been prevented from learning how to make a living to support themselves. At the time of separation all access to financial resources were stopped and the children removed from her care. These women reported severe alienation of affection.

It makes one grateful to have laws that protect human rights and enforce a better way of resolving conflict than a winner-take all approach.

How common is PA and PAS?

When parents first separate there is often parent alienation. For example, due to the anxiety of the mother, she is likely to say indirectly to a child that he or she is not safe with the father.

She might say:

"Call me as soon as you get there to let me know you are okay."
"If you get scared, you call me right away. Okay?"
"I'll come get you if you want to come home."

Usually this level of alienation dies down after the separating parents get used to changes brought on by the separation and move on with their lives.

However, in rare cases, the anxiety not only doesn't calm down, it escalates. PAS parents are psychologically fragile. When things are going their way, they can hold themselves together. When they are threatened however, they can become fiercely entrenched in preserving what they see is rightfully theirs.

Fortunately, only a small percentage end up in this level of conflict.

Why do PAS parents act like they do?

I believe that PAS parents have become stuck in the first stage of child development, where survival skills are learned.

To them, having total control over their child is a life and death matter. Because they don't understand how to please other people, any effort to do so always has strings attached. They don't give; they only know how to take. They don't play by the rules and are not likely to obey a court order.

Descriptions that are commonly used to describe severe cases of PAS are that the alienating parent is unable to "individuate" (a psychological term used when the person is unable to see the child as a separate human being from him or herself). They are often described as being "overly involved with the child" or "enmeshed".

The parent may be diagnosed as narcissistic (self-centred), where they presume that they have a special entitlement to whatever they want. They think that there are rules in life, but only for other people, not for them.

Also, they may be called a sociopath, which means a person who has no moral conscience. These are people who are unable to have empathy or compassion for others. They are unable to see a situation from another person's point of view, especially their child's point of view. They don't distinguish between telling the truth and lying in the way that others do.

In spite of admonitions from judges and mental health professionals to stop their alienation, they can't. The prognosis for severely alienating parents is very poor. It is unlikely that they are able to "get it." It is also unlikely that they will ever stop trying to perpetuate the alienation. This is a gut wrenching survival issue to them.

How does the child get involved in PAS?

The targeted parent needs to understand what has happened to what as once an affectionate and loving child who is now unexplainably hostile. Remember Gardner's definition stated earlier, "the disorder wasn't only brainwashing or programming by a parent, but was confounded by what he calls *self-created contributions by the child in support of the alienating parent's campaign of denigration against the targeted parent*." It isn't PAS in the severe form of this disorder, unless the child has crossed over and joined up with the alienating parent. The child shares the alienating parent's psychosis. How does this happen?

At birth, children are totally reliant on a parent, usually the mother, for having all of their needs met. It is part of normal child development to be enmeshed with their primary caregiver, and very young children do not have a separate identity from this caregiver.

One of the mother's roles is to help the child develop as a separate person, therefore, infancy and childhood become a series of tasks of learning how to become independent. For example, learning to putting oneself back to sleep, eating, toilet training and caring for one's hygiene.

Instead of promoting this independence, the alienating parent encourages continued dependence. The parent may insist on sleeping with the child, feeding the child ("It's easier if I do it"), and taking care of these rites of passage longer than normal child development calls for. This "spoiling" may not feel right to the child, but they do not have enough ego strength to do anything about it.

A PAS mother can't imagine that the father is capable of planning the child's time while in his care. Therefore, she arranges several things for the child to do while at the father's house. One of the most common ways of doing this is to sign the child up for on-going lessons without permission from the father.

The parent may even decree whom the child can and cannot see, particularly specific members of the child's extended family on the father's side. The mother desperately wants control over the time when the child isn't with her.

One of the most unusual situations that I ran into was the father who picked up his sons at 9:00 a.m. on a Saturday for the weekend. He discovered that his very excited boys had their hearts set on going to Disneyland for the day, when this idea had never crossed his mind.

One theory about why a mother will act this way is that when a father takes his share of joint custody, it is like asking her to give away part of her body. One mother said, "He is going to remove my right arm and take it for the weekend." It feels like the mother has lost a profound part of who she is as a person. She feels fractured, pulled apart.

Why is PAS a double bind for the child?

When children spend time with the father, and enjoy it, they are put into a double bind. Clearly, they cannot tell the mother that dad treats them well or that they had fun together. They want to bond with the father, but don't dare. They figure out on which side the bread is buttered (who has the power), and their survival needs tug at them. Therefore, children will tell the mother about everything they didn't enjoy about time spent with the father, which will add to her belief that they don't like to be with him. These children feel that they must protect the mother. The same is true when the alienator is the father. The child will avoid expressing their affectionate feelings for the mother to him.

Family volatility

These are volatile families. The father may have indeed spanked a child, or lashed out at the mother physically or emotionally. An isolated incidence can turn into a holocaust. One father spanked his rebellious child and ended up in jail on child abuse charges, followed by a six week trial to determine his guilt. The jury returned with a not guilty verdict in 20 minutes. The verdict didn't end it as far as the mother was concerned, however.

The alienating parent's hatred can have no bounds. The severest form will bring out every horrible allegation known, including claims of domestic violence, stalking and the sexual molestation of the child. Many fathers say that there have been repeated calls to the Department of Family and Child Services alleging child abuse and neglect.

In most cases the investigators report that they found nothing wrong. However, the indoctrinating parent feels that these reports are not fabrications, but very, very real. She can describe the horror of what happen in great detail. Regardless of the actual truth, in her mind, it did happen.

Most of the alienated fathers that I work with are continually befuddled by her lying. "How can she lie like that?" They don't realize that these lies are not based on rational thinking. They are incapable of understanding the difference between what is true and what they want to be true. A vital part of fighting PAS is to understand the severity of the psychological disturbance that is the source of it.

Intergenerational patterns

What makes this problem very complicated is that PAS is often intergenerational in dysfunctional families. Almost always the alienator has people within the family who support the alienation. It might be the mother, father or grandparent who encourage fighting. They are likely to support the parent financially or even provide massive amounts of money to fund litigation. This is further proof to the PAS parent that he or she is justified in what he/she does.

When a child is placed in the role of the parent's therapist

Alienation advances even further when the alienating parent uses the child as a personal therapist. The child is told about every miserable experience and negative feeling about the alienated parent with great specificity. The child, who is already enmeshed with the parent because his or her own identity is still undefined, easily absorbs the parent's negativity. They become aligned with this parent and feel that they need to be the protector of the alienating parent.

What happens to the child when you can't stop PAS?

Obviously, without anyone to stop the alienation from progressing, the child will become estranged from the alienated parent. The relationship with this parent will eventually be severed. It is doubtful that, without psychological intervention as the child grows, he or she will ever understand what happened.

The child's primary role model will be the maladaptive, dysfunctional parent. He or she will not have the benefit of growing up with the most well-adjusted parent and all that this parent can contribute to enrich the child's life. Many of these children come to experience serious psychiatric problems.

Will they ever grow up and realize what happened to them? Without someone who can recognize the syndrome and counsel them about it, it isn't likely that they will ever figure it out. However, there have been exceptions where the child and the alienated parent have been successfully reunified later in life.

How can good intentions backfire?

Those people who are typically called upon to handle such difficult situations, such as the police, social workers, attorneys or psychologists assume that what the frightened mother is saying is true. These things DO happen. There are men who are seriously disturbed, violent, out of control sexually, and stalk, who are rightfully feared. The mother is very convincing in her desperation and vivid in her descriptions. The clincher is that the alienated child collaborates with the mother by saying, "Yes, I am afraid of my father." "Yes, my father did touch me down there." "Yes, he does beat me." What would you do if you were faced with having to decide how to protect a child in such a situation?

Therapists

Some therapists don't realize the severity and depth of the problem. In fact, they may unwittingly side with the alienating parent and even testify in court that the child is afraid of the alienated parent. This can be a serious stumbling block in getting an accurate diagnosis. Indeed, it can tip the scale into the alienating parent's agenda and do real damage.

Our courts, social services and mental health workers are all committed to stop child abuse and neglect when they see it occurring. Unfortunately, in PAS situations a dramatic and loud complaint from the alienating parent often ends up being acted upon without an investigation as to the accuracy of the allegation. This frequently removes the alienated parent from the children and allows the alienating parent considerable additional time to proceed with the alienation.

By the time all of the evaluations are in place and the case is heard by the court, considerable damage has been done to the child. It is an irony that the very people we turn to for help in such a difficult situation can often be those who most contribute to allowing the on-going abuse and neglect of the child to continue.

What can be done about the problem?

First, it takes a sophisticated mental health professional to be able to identify that PAS is occurring. Most forensic evaluators such as psychiatrists and clinical psychologists have studied the disorder and are able to recognize it.

Forensic evaluators diagnose PAS by having the parents take a battery of psychological tests, doing a detailed case history and by observation. They make recommendations as to what to do. After the evaluator has written a report on the family and made recommendations, nothing will happen to resolve the crisis without court intervention.

The alienated parent has to take the report to a judge who must then be convinced that the child is being alienated and that it is not in their best interest to stay in such an environment.

It is rare however that judges have any degree of mental health training. They most often learn about PAS from the bench. It usually takes several trips to court to point out how badly a child is being treated before a judge is willing to act.

How are PAS cases resolved legally?

Judges are inevitably conservative in their orders. Even when the evidence is overwhelming that the alienation is occurring, the court order may still end up saying, "the parents are to make joint decisions about the child's welfare," when this is impossible to do.

This is further evidence that the judge doesn't understand the magnitude of the problem. The judge in one of the most severe PAS cases I worked on was from the old school. He was tired of having the litigants continue to appear before him. One day he said, "Why don't the two of you go out in the hallway and kiss and make up." This is an example of how frustrating these cases are for judges. Indeed, these are the hardest cases to decide.

Judges have been slow to place serious sanctions on the alienating parent. If there is no threat of severe fines, jail time or sole custody to the targeted parent, the chances are remote that the out-of-control parent can be stopped.

It usually takes a dramatic situation where court orders are broken to force the court to change primary custody. Often it is only a matter of time before alienating parents become desperate and their unstable mental health gets the better of them. People in an official position start to recognize the alienating parent as being out of line, and become supportive of the targeted parent.

In one case, the 9 and 4 year old daughters were abducted and presumed to be on their way to Australia through an underground group that hides women who are victims of domestic violence, often of a sexual nature and where the father is stalking. The girls were missing for 3 months and found in another county where they were waiting for final arrangements to be made before their departure. When the police broke into the house at 3:00 a.m., they found the girls sleeping with their mother. They had been given boy's names, clothes, haircuts and their hair was dyed. They were not allowed contact with anyone outside of their hiding place, not even to go to school. The oldest child had strep throat and the youngest was seriously withdrawn.

In another case, the mother could no longer convince the social workers, the police or the Court about her allegations. She was known to be unstable because she had "cried wolf" too many times. She abducted her daughter to Utah. She told officials there that the courts where she lived were protecting a proven child molester. The press was called. After she was interviewed; there was a virtual feeding frenzy as the father's photograph and the story was on all the local news networks.

A big part of the problem was that the seven year old girl, said "Yes" when asked if her father had molested her. Even though this had already been disproved by forensic evaluators, she was still confused.

Can the alienation of children be reversed?

As children get older, the alienation can be reversed with proper psychological care. However, it won't work if the alienating parent is not contained. In the last case described above, the mother had severely limited visiting rights. She had remarried and had a new child; however, she still regularly calls the police to report the father for abuse. Presently, the daughter resides with her father, receives weekly therapy and hates the police. She gradually understands how disturbed her mother is In the former case, where the mother was kidnapping the

I fought this battle for about five years and walked away last year. I am happier now than I was then and expect to be even more so next year at this time. My four were/are teens and young adults. I was always so deeply hurt by the disgust, contempt and disdain, while their father walked on water. He who had rarely made it home in time to join us for dinner, he who was not taking them to gymnastics classes, swimming lessons, camps, dr appts, etc while they were growing up. It is very sad because I can see how he is using them and manipulating them with promises of hefty life insurance. They all still live with him! - I suspect they will for a long time since he is too lonely to allow them a way to move out. Instead, some of them have boy and girlfriends who have moved in as well. Our youngest daughter - in high school - is easily manipulated and he uses her for backrubs and other physical things I would consider to be inappropriate. Remember though, he is a saint and I am the worst parent on the planet. I don't see her or any of them as victims - he is their choice for parent of the year.I merely exited the stage and let them enjoy their choice.I have a wonderful few dogs who are more deserving of my time and affection. My teen and young adult children actually saved me a great deal of money by pushing me out of their lives. And there is some relief to do it early on in their lives as well. I won't know any grandchildren since I am out of their lives before any are born, I won't be second place at any weddings as I was at the Scouting and high school graduation ceremonies/events, and I am nearly completely free of their hatred, as well as the sadness and despair that felt so overwhelming last year at this time.

I can admire those of you willing to stick it out but I am just not seeing any change down the road. My Chihuahua has an entire wardrobe and will never turn on me like my children did. I will be fine. I hope they have nice lives

My partner's son packed up a left our home about a month ago while we were not home. It was a total shock for us as he did not spend much time at his mother's. He left a note in his bedroom saying that he was very stressed and that we had too high expectations for him but at the end said that he still loved him as his father. After he left we only talked to him a few times as he was avoiding us but now he will not talk to us at all nor any of my partner's family. We are all shocked and this is soo unlike him and we are all very concerned for him. My partner does believe that his ex has talked about him very poorly in front of the kids (two boys) since the separation (which was over approximately 8 or more years ago) and even showed them court documents after a 50/50 custody agreement. She even took her son to court with her at one point. I'm sure she had said and done many more things but just giving you idea of the type of things she had done. It is heart breaking as these kids have been in my life now over 5 years and I treat them like my own. I don't understand how she can be so selfish and not realize the damage that she is doing to her children's mental health. What is even more frustrating is that myself and my partner feel like there is absolutely nothing we can do to prevent this or help his son. The other son is following the 50/50 custody agreement of a week with us and a week with his mother and he seems to be doing fine. We have been asking him some questions but not too many as he seems to not want to get involved (like rat on his mother.) Anyways hope to get some advice here on this situation and if there are any other avenues we can take to help

I'm a 57 year old mom of 3 daughters that I raised. I was their class moms, girl scout leaders, soccer moms, dance mom, all while holding down a full time job. They were 3,6 and 8 when we divorced. He was a decent guy back then, just not a good husband and we divorced amicably. A year later he began dating his 2nd wife. I saw a change in the way he treated me. And I heard from the kids there was lots of mom bashing taking place. I told the girls to let it "go in one ear and out the other". I tried to talk to him about it but I no longer recognized who he was. So I would respond with answers, when the kids came home angry, like "do you live with them? Then don't worry about it." or "Isn't it sad they have nothing else to talk about?" I truly thought he was damaging his relationship with his kids. Fast forward 15 years and they are 19, 22 and 24. I only have a relationship with my 19 yr old. The other two never see me, one hates me and the oldest has no feelings for me whatsoever. I often wish I was dead. I know I was a good and loving mother, they all had huge scholarships to top colleges and were overachievers. My 22 yr old is fighting for her life - stage 4 lymphoma bone cancer. And she still won't have anything to do with me. She has not spoken to me in 3 years when she had "an opportunity to be closer to her father" and when I asked her to put our differences aside (I never understood what they were, she just came home from college her sophomore year and hated me, after we were so close while she was growing up) during her war on cancer. She said no. She blames me for being misdiagnosed twice while in her father's care, I didn't even know anything about it. My 24 yr old only contacts me to tell me to leave my 22 year old alone. In all my life I never thought this was possible. I have a relationship with my youngest which I am eternally grateful for but it docsn't take away from the agony of not having my other daughter's in my life. I am also fighting cancer, malt lymphoma in my stomach. But not nearly as serious as my daughters. I don't know how to go on, I just get up every day and put one-foot in front of the other. But in all honestly, the desire to live has gone right out the window. I feel all I do is cry. How could this happen? I feel like I've been in a nightmare the last 3 years there is no waking up from. To date, through my daughter's brain surgery to her diagnosis, her father has not once contacted me. It's like he just wiped me out of their lives, in his mind

Gardner described PAS as a preoccupation by the child with criticism and deprecation of a parent.[20] Gardner stated that PAS occurs when, in the context of child custody disputes, one parent deliberately or unconsciously attempts to alienate a child from the other parent.[21] According to Gardner, PAS is characterized by a cluster of eight symptoms that appear in the child. These include a campaign of denigration and hatred against the targeted parent; weak, absurd, or frivolous rationalizations for this deprecation and hatred; lack of the usual ambivalence about the targeted parent; strong assertions that the decision to reject the parent is theirs alone (the "independent-thinker phenomenon"); reflexive support of the favored parent in the conflict; lack of guilt over the treatment of the alienated parent; use of borrowed scenarios and phrases from the alienating parent; and the denigration not just of the targeted parent but also to that parent's extended family and friends.[13][18][22] Despite frequent citations of these factors in scientific literature, "the value ascribed to these factors has not been explored with professionals in the field."[23]

Gardner and others have divided PAS into mild, moderate and severe levels. The number and severity of the eight symptoms displayed increase through the different levels. The recommendations for management differ according to the severity level of the child's symptoms. While a diagnosis of PAS is made based on the child's symptoms, Gardner stated that any change in custody should be based primarily on the symptom level of the alienating parent.[24] In mild cases, there is some parental programming against the targeted parent, but little or no disruption of visitation, and Gardner did not recommend court-ordered visitation. In moderate cases, there is more parental programming and greater resistance to visits with the targeted parent. Gardner recommended that primary custody remain with the programming parent if the brainwashing was expected to be discontinued, but if not, that custody should be transferred to the targeted parent. In addition, therapy with the child to stop alienation and remediate the damaged relationship with the targeted parent was recommended. In severe cases, children display most or all of the 8 symptoms, and will refuse steadfastly to visit the targeted parent, including threatening to run away or commit suicide if the visitation is forced. Gardner recommended that the child be removed from the alienating parent's home into a transition home before moving into the home of the targeted parent. In addition, therapy for the child is recommended.[1][22][24] Gardner's proposed intervention for moderate and severe PAS, including court-ordered transfer to the alienated parent, fines, house arrest, incarceration, have been critiqued for their punitive nature towards the alienating parent and alienated child, and for the risk of abuse of power and violation of their civil rights.[25][26] With time, Gardner revised his views and expressed less support for the most aggressive management strategies.[25]

My husband (target) is at the beginning stages of parental alienation by his ex wife (alienator). My husband is father of three children with his ex, 7, 8 and 11. We have them every other day, take them to gymnastics and soccer every weekend, make it a point to maintain as dependable a schedule as possible, and always make time for bonding time. Our motto is "consistency" and "balance" for the kiddos. I would like to think that my husband and I do everything in our power to insure the kiddos are well balanced, healthy, and loved when they are with us. My husband is without a doubt the most loving, honest, and wonderful father I have been blessed to witness. He does everything for his kids.

Now for the point, my husbands ex was never on good terms with us. She was extremely jealous and hostile at the beginning of our relationship. Although she loves her kids, she often does not bath them, never seems to have time to do homework them, feeds them chicken nuggets for dinner and cupcakes for breakfast, often leaves the kids at her mothers to go out on days she is allegedly has them, etc. My husband recently went through his 11 yr. old son's phone to find frantic text messages to his mother asking her when she will be home, he does not feel safe at his grandmother's, and begging her to come home at 2am. He also discovered the fact that his ex will text his son about how his father called her and that his father is angry at him and her, and why did he tell his dad that she left them at their grandma's, etc. Essentially she does not keep their "co-parenting" conversations to herself and expresses arguments to the kids that they having. Painting a very hostile and false picture of my husband. In short, she is manipulating the kids to love her chaotic, materialistic, and unorganized world, making my husband out to be a tyrant of a father who abuses their mother verbally.

There are so many other things, I could write a book. My husband and I are at out wits end. We have noticed that the kids have been acting differently since she a new bf in the picture (who is a complete rude low life). They have been distant, cry when we go to pick them up from their mother's, fight tooth and nail over homework and bath, telling my husband that "mom is better", personally attacking each other over things they never used to, and count down the minutes until they go back to their mothers. It has taken a deep toll on my husband who cherishes every minute he has with the kids. I am not saying we are perfect but we live and breath for these kiddos and their mother showed a less than stellar performance in her mother duties for as long as I've known her. Why do the kids cling to her and reject us? It's beginning to break our hearts..

Any advice is greatly appreciated

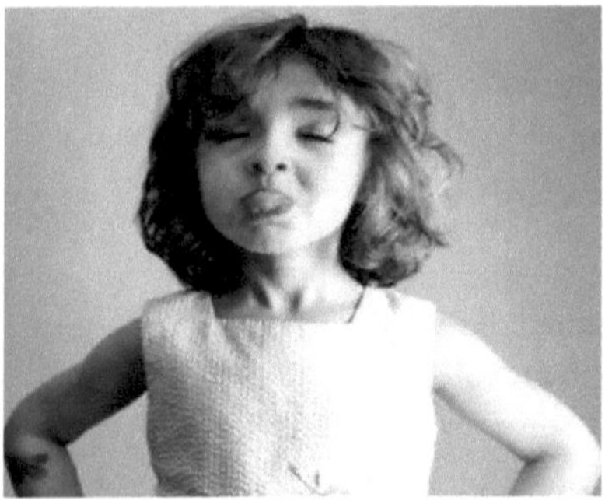

What do you want from me am not coming with you?

Parental alienation occurs often, but not always, in the context of divorce and custody battles. No one knows how many children are exposed to parental alienation or show signs of the parental alienation syndrome, but we do know that it can happen to mothers as well as fathers, to custodial parents as well as non-custodial parents and to kids as young as toddlers or as old as teens. It is marked by sudden changes in your child's interactions with you and you'll see new personality traits begin to emerge.

Here are some attitudes and behaviours to watch for:

Leave me alone. Your child is filled with animosity toward you. When confronted and reminded of the good times you two once shared, she insists you two NEVER had a good relationship although you know that is not true. Suddenly, your once-loving and affectionate child seems to fear and, in some cases, despise you. He may even be reluctant to share a meal with you as though merely being in your presence is unbearable. When you question this, your child gives you frivolous and absurd reasons for this newfound negativity.

It's all your fault. Your child acts as if the other parent can do no wrong. Everything the other parent does is perfect in his eyes something your child never seemed to feel about your ex during the marriage. Your child seems to forgive your ex even the most inexcusable behaviour while ridiculing you for minor flaws and infractions.

Yeah, what he said. Your child consistently sides with your ex. And it seems she is following a script when she is talking about you, using some of the same labels your ex has used to describe you. He will repeat the same words and phrases, as if he is relying on words that are not his own and may have been rehearsed beforehand.

Family ties no longer bind.Your child shows no guilt about her shabby treatment of you. And she not only rejects you, but by extension, your family as well. Formerly beloved aunts, uncles, cousins, and grandparents are now shunned. And your child doesn't want to attend important family events such asweddings, reunions, even funerals.

Influence? What influence?Your child vehemently denies being influenced by your ex. When you note that he is using words and phrases that appear to parrot the other parent, your child dismisses you. In fact, he scoffs at the idea of being coached by anyone.

Since then, everything has changed. She has essentially removed me from all family activities. I do work a lot and cannot be with the family as much as I would like, but she has made it quite clear that she does not want me to be involved in the things she does with our 10 and 13 year old daughters. Now my daughters barely even acknowledge my presence in the room. If I happen to be home when they leave for school, they don't say good bye to me before they leave. When I go to tuck them into bed at night, they recoil from me. When I get home from work and say hello, give them a kiss, and ask them how their day was, I am lucky to get a "fine" from them. When I ask them if they want to do something fun with me, they always say "No"....unless my wife says she is interested. Then they say OK. On top of that, when the kids disrespect me verbally or by their actions in the presence of my wife, she does not correct that behavior. For me, this is the most horrible existence I could have ever imagined.

My wife suffers from Depression and for years I have had to walk on eggshells, turn the other cheek, and hope that "tomorrow will be a better day". I have (and continue to) check my anger at the door....but every once in awhile it boils over, and then I look like the bad guy...so now I think my kids just see me as "the guy who makes mommy sad". And I am sure she helps to reinforce that belief.

I do not know what to do. If I stand firm against her, I am afraid my kids will be more resolved than ever to hate me even more. If I let it continue, I validate their behavior. Her parents are good people, but refuse to get involved....she is an only child (her only brother was killed in an industrial accident 13 years ago....10 days after our first daughter was born). So, in her parents' eyes, she can do no wrong....and they will not stand up to her at all.

Despite all this, I still love my wife, and hope for a day when she will smile every morning and be happy. All I want is for us to be happy, and to have my kids hug me again and say "Hi Daddy, I love you". I would love to take them somewhere for the day by myself for a little one on one (which my wife has never ever allowed me to do in our 13 years of parenthood. I think that thinking comes from her brother's death (they were very close) happening so closely to our first daughter's birth....she is so utterly afraid that something bad will happen to her kids if she is not there to protect them. She will only trust them with her Mom and Dad.But now I am rambling on. I promised myself I would be direct and to the point...but I got lost in all of this. Apologies.

Ultimately, what I want and need is to have my kids like me and want to be with me again. Anybody out there have any advice for me

I find a lot of comfort in reading these comments. Of course, that's because misery loves company...

Sadly, I am a mother of two girls and I have been greatly afflicted by PAS. I have two, grown adult daughters who stayed w/their dad after our divorce; they are now 23 and 25 yrs old. The alienation has been in full force for over 10 yrs now and my girls now have the "independent thinking" that Amy Baker refers to in her books. Meaning, their father no longer has to malign me to them constantly, they've picked up on ways to denigrate me on their own now and see his same short comings in me, so he just sits back now and gloats as their contempt towards me flourishes more and more each day.

Recently, I fell on hard times (I was a victim of a crime and lost everything that I owned) so I had to leave my own residence and return to live (albeit temporarily) w/my ex and daughters in this hostile household. That's a LONG story and the result was not something that either he nor I wanted to have happen. (We short of co-own this house; another long story...) I had nowhere else to go on the spur of the moment, yet we'd been divorced for 4 yrs prior to this new upheaval.

Prior to this tragedy, I had begun to make progress w/my girls once I was independent of their malicious father and out on my own. They had even begun to complain to me about him yet I would just listen and not gossip but that was very hard NOT to do (I sure had to bite my lip!).

Now, these two daughters are almost violent to me. I have tried to explain my temporary set back and dire circumstances to them but they want nothing to do w/me. I was the family bread winner for many years throughout our marriage. When I was recently diagnosed with cancer, my youngest told me that she hopes I die soon and that no one loves me. This was such an awful stab to the heart and I cried for days about this. Having to endure their vicious slings and arrows is much worse then the crime committed against me by a stalker AND my cancer diagnosis, combined. We have a family dog whom I love very much that my daughters try to keep away from me because he often seeks me out, much to their chagrin. When he enters my room, they scream and yell for him and actually chastise the animal once he responds. My daughters tell me that they want me to "rot and burn in hell" as their father passively stands back and says nothing about this horrifically abhorrent behavior.

Today is my eldest daughters birthday. Both she and her boyfriend along w/my other daughter and ex husband are about to go out to dinner to celebrate. I will remain home much like Cinderella was; left to clean out the fireplace. I don't know how my eldest can celebrate her birthday independent of even thinking of me since I was an active participant in that event 25 yrs ago. I told her just to pretend that she was left on the doorstep of her father's home 25 yrs ago by the stork.

I must say I'm a rare parent who does NOT intend to try and heal this rift once I'm out on my own again. Going through cancer and almost dying after two surgeries and not once having my daughters ask how I was feeling when I returned from the hospital has hardened my heart toward them considerably. When the "independent thinking" unfolds, the alienated parent no longer even blames the ex spouse entirely anymore for this behavior - the children have their own set of ideas and opinions that form against us each day so we're left to deflect and defend against them independent of the alienator. I just want to be free of this alienation toxicity and don't care which of those 3 people is targeting me with it.Have any other parents on this site had to turn their backs upon their children as the years have gone by just to maintain their sanity and their health?

In order to live out the rest of my life in peace and avoid future heartaches (like being alienated from eventual grandchildren, etc) I find that with the limited time left in life I don't want to deal with their vile temperaments and growing hostilities. I can choose to be miserable and continue chasing after them for crumbs of acceptance OR I can disengage and focus on being with people who are uplifting, happy and kind.

Sadly, that's not such a hard chose to make in life when a person's reached the end of their rope

adly, I am a mother of two girls and I have been greatly afflicted by PAS. I have two, grown adult daughters who stayed w/their dad after our divorce; they are now 23 and 25 yrs old. The alienation has been in full force for over 10 yrs now and my girls now have the "independent thinking" that Amy Baker refers to in her books. Meaning, their father no longer has to malign me to them constantly, they've picked up on ways to denigrate me on their own now and see his same short comings in me, so he just sits back now and gloats as their contempt towards me flourishes more and more each day.

Recently, I fell on hard times (I was a victim of a crime and lost everything that I owned) so I had to leave my own residence and return to live (albeit temporarily) w/my ex and daughters in this hostile household. That's a LONG story and the end result was not something that either he nor I wanted to have happen. (We short of co-own this house; another long story...) I had nowhere else to go on the spur of the moment, yet we'd been divorced for 4 yrs prior to this new upheaval.

Prior to this tragedy, I had begun to make progress w/my girls once I was independent of their malicious father and out on my own. They had even begun to complain to me about him yet I would just listen and not gossip but that was very hard NOT to do (I sure had to bite my lip!).

Now, these two daughters are almost violent to me. I have tried to explain my temporary set back and dire circumstances to them but they want nothing to do w/me. I was the family bread winner for many years throughout our marriage. When I was recently diagnosed with cancer, my youngest told me that she hopes I die soon and that no one loves me. This was such an awful stab to the heart and I cried for days about this. Having to endure their vicious slings and arrows is much worse then the crime committed against me by a stalker AND my cancer diagnosis, combined.

We have a family dog whom I love very much that my daughters try to keep away from me because he often seeks me out, much to their chagrin. When he enters my room, they scream and yell for him and actually chastise the animal once he responds. My daughters tell me that they want me to "rot and burn in hell" as their father passively stands back and says nothing about this horrifically abhorrent behavior.

Today is my eldest daughters birthday. Both she and her boyfriend along w/my other daughter and ex husband are about to go out to dinner to celebrate. I will remain home much like Cinderella was; left to clean out the fireplace. I don't know how my eldest can celebrate her birthday independent of even thinking of me since I was an active participant in that event 25 yrs. ago. I told her just to pretend that she was left on the doorstep of her father's home 25 yrs. ago by the stork.

I must say I'm a rare parent who does NOT intend to try and heal this rift once I'm out on my own again. Going through cancer and almost dying after two surgeries and not once having my daughters ask how I was feeling when I returned from the hospital has hardened my heart toward them considerably. When the "independent thinking" unfolds, the alienated parent no longer even blames the ex-spouse entirely anymore for this behaviour - the children have their own set of ideas and opinions that form against us each day so we're left to deflect and defend against them independent of the alienator. I just want to be free of this alienation toxicity and don't care which of those 3 people is targeting me with it.

Have any other parents on this site had to turn their backs upon their children as the years have gone by just to maintain their sanity and their health?

In order to live out the rest of my life in peace and avoid future heartaches (like being alienated from eventual grandchildren, etc) I find that with the limited time left in life I don't want to deal with their vile temperaments and growing hostilities. I can choose to be miserable and continue chasing after them for crumbs of acceptance OR I can disengage and focus on being with people who are uplifting, happy and kind

Parental Alienation IS child abuse and emotional abuse ... the following is an outline prepared from the personal experiences of many along with much professional input and attempts to explain in laymans terms various aspects of Parental Alienation.

Parental alienation should not be confused with parental alienation syndrome (PAS) as one is the act of and the other is the result of and in Australia many courts refer to parental alienation as "alignment", parental alienation must have been practiced to have alignment happen.

Parental Alienation is the act of a parent or person coaching/convincing the Children to "break away" from the other parent by way of brainwashing the Children into thinking badly of the targeted Parent often to the point of them refusing to having anything or little to do with that parent, in most cases the Children actually not only believe the words of the Alienator unconditionally at the time but are also coached in such a way as to believe that it is themselves that have made the decission to not love or want to see the other Parent.

Alienators are cunning in their ways and will do almost anything to achieve their goal and this often includes making false allegations of harm to the Children supposedly by the targeted parent that in most cases involves expensive court time and much stress, some targeted parents even give up the fight due to not having the means to meet the expense or choosing not to endure the stress and this is what the alienator wants to happen as it usually results in the targeted parent exiting from the lives of the Children.

The alienator claims to love the Children whilst at the same time their actions are significantly detracting from the Childrens rights, best interests and long term emotional stability, the alienator usually does not care about those things, just to reach their perverted goal at almost any cost, they are acomplished liars and a disgrace to parenthood and there can be many reasons for their actions, mostly perverted and or extremely selfish.

The alienators in most cases know all to well what they are doing to the children and to the targeted parent but once they start they are driven to continue, even into becomming obsessive against the targeted parent ... all at the chidrens cost, alienators will never admit to fault and after some time can even believe themselves that they are not at fault, many even exhibit the signs of various disorders but refuse the sugestions, even professional, indicating such, some back off when they have acieved their goals and others continue for years but in their own minds they are the innocent ones but one thing does not change and that is they are emotionally abusing the children, they are abusing their own children.

The children are "under the spell" of the alienator and especially when young, follow all direction from and adopt all the opinions of the alienator and it is important to remember that ... whatever the children do or say it is not of their own free mind, it is what they are coached/instructed into saying and doing and it is only when they are mature enough that, with or without intervention, they have any chance of working out the truth and discovering their own thoughts and feelings.

Dr. Douglas Darnall in his book Divorce Casualties: Protecting Your Children from Parental Alienation, describes three categories of PA:

MILD: Naïve alienators

Naïve alienators are ignorant of what they are doing and are willing to be educated and change.

MODERATE: Active alienators

When triggered, active alienators lose control of appropriate boundaries. They go ballistic. When they calm down, they don't want to admit that they were out of control.

SEVERE: Obsessed alienators

Obsessed alienators operate from a delusional system where every cell of their body is committed to destroying the other parent's relationship with the child.

In the case of the Obsessed alienator, no treatment exists other than removing the child from their influence.

Here are some scenarios that could be by themselves issues or combined together to make these alienators who they are and why they do what they do.

The alienator is so filled with anger, rage and hatred that they cannot see any further past that and their whole entire world is wrapped around making sure the other person hurts as much as they do. It is like they are blinded by their anger and hatred.

They were raised in a home where one of their parents was an alienator and it is the only thing they know about relationships, that is one person controls everyone and if you do not have control, then you are nothing. So they would not know how to have a relationship any other way nor would they know how to handle it any other way when they loose control over everyone, because to not be in total control means that you are a looser.

The alienator could have such low self-esteem that anyone putting them down or any inference that anything they were involved in was a failure, such as their marriage, would set them off, fighting to defend their honour and reputation. They are so protective of their image, that they will do anything to make sure that they stay looking like the perfect person and destroy everyone else around them to maintain that image.

The alienators own parents put them down constantly and told them they would never amount to much and when their own marriage fails, they are desperate to prove their parents were wrong and will do anything to make it look like it was not their fault.

The alienator's have warped views of themselves from low self- esteem issues. It puts them in such a fragile state of fear that they are no good unless they are seen as all good.

The alienator cannot accept responsibility for their actions and blame them on everyone else because how could they possibly be wrong. Everyone else is wrong.

The alienator is so narcissistic in their beliefs that they are never wrong, to protect that image, they must make sure that they are always on top and that it is everyone's problem or fault.

The alienator was never taught to take responsibility for their own actions and to be humble when they have made a mistake. They were raised that they could do no wrong, just like their own parent/s could do not wrong and thus it is everyone else who is wrong and so Instead they were raised to blame everyone else for their mistakes.

The alienator is so terrified of loosing their children that they have to paint this perfect picture of themselves and make the other person look so bad, to ensure that they do not loose their children and control.

The alienator is so terrified that they are not lovable that they force others to love them.

The alienator is not a real good sharer. In other words, they do not know how to share love and happiness. Maybe because they had to share their parents and never got to understand that sharing is a good thing and feels really good to do.

The alienator often believes that by gaining total control of the children prior to any property settlement that they will benefit financially from same and that they will recieve maximum ongoing financial support from agencies like child support and social security should they have significant custody of the children.

It is usually the alienator that ends the relationship with the other parent and looks to justify their decission to friends and family by making out the other parent was at fault and not worthy of any consideration in the process, they cannot accept responsability for their own actions.

The alienator may have a disorder such as borderline personality disorder.

Eight Behaviors of a Child Being Manipulated;

Expletives and Bad-mouthing: The child denigrates the alienated parent with foul language and severe oppositional behaviour.

Excuses without Foundation: The child offers weak, absurd or frivolous reasons for his or her anger.

Consistently Negative: The child is sure of him or herself, never swaying from a negative connotation. He/she doesn't demonstrate confused emotions (i.e. love and hate) for the alienated parent, only the negative hate.

Self-righteous: The child exhorts that he or she alone came up with ideas of denigration. The "independent-thinker" phenomenon is where the child asserts that no one told him to do this.

Protective: supports and feels a need to protect the alienating parent.

Lack of Empathy: the child does not demonstrate guilt over cruelty towards the alienated parent.

Lying & embellishing: the child uses borrowed scenarios or vividly describes situations that he or she could not have experienced.

Anger: Animosity is spread to the friends and/or extended family of the alienated parent.

The alienators "tools of trade".

Many alienators will not come out and degrade the targeted openly (many do), some use more subtle methods and when you think you have heard it all more come to light, although some use only a few others use many, here are some;

Sympathy ... alienators often use sympathy to gain the loyalty of the children, this can be as simple as "he/she left us with no money and does not care about us", sympathy from friends and family is important also as the alienator sees this as loyalty, support and justification for their actions ... "I cry and miss you terribly when you stay over at his/her place", not hard to guess what the children are left with on this one, they do not want to see the alienator hurt, anyone for that matter but the targeted do not usually say things like this so the children do not think the alienator does miss them or get hurt when they are not with the targeted.

Emotional support ... by enlisting the childrens emotional support the children become loyal at the cost of the other parent, here the alienator sets out to have the children feel sorry for the alienator and to have negative attitudes towards the targeted, the children are made to feel they have to support the alienator and in many cases are also made to feel that if they continue to love the targeted that the alienator will be let down.

False allegations of abuse ... one of the favourites, this can be and mostly is sexual abuse against the children, this is a biggy and hits hard to the innocent targeted parent and often results in that parent not seeing the children for some time or only under supervision after some time and then court proceedings all of which are expensive and emotionally draining, here the alienator is hoping the targeted will just give up and walk away or to give in to unreasonable demands, usually financial.

Control ... the alienator has to feel in control and will do almost anything to get it and an example here is "if you do that then this may happen (bad)", leaving the children to make the decission that the alienator wanted all along.

The power of Suggestive comments ... "you make sure that he/she looks after you when you are there, make sure that you get enough food and tell me if you don't", when a child hears this type of comment they immediately become suspicious and concerned with the targeted parent, and will often report negatively about their stay to the alienator knowing the alienator is expecting it.

Trying to buy love ... the alienator will most likely have the children prepared that should you give them something that they don't have at the alienators place their comment will be "you cannot buy our love with gifts", the real side of this is the children think they do not love you and that you cannot secure their love, the alienator will have gone to great lengths on this one so that whatever you do they may well refuse to love you.

Name changing ... the alienator in many case's tries to change the childrens surnames and has the children believe that their new name is a better name and possibly that your surname has a bad reputation and that is why the change, the alienator will have justified the attempt to change their name to the children in some way.

"Does he/she treat and speak to you properly" ... a simple thing like you raising your voice will be and indication to the children that you don't, by the time the alienator has finished with this one you will have shouted at them and the alienator will have said things like "if he/she shouted at you then he/she does not respect or love you", it is not the alienator making the decission about you, the children based on what the alienator has explained will make the decission that you do not respect or love them. This is a favourite method used by an alienator, just supply a well crafted and pointed basis for a decission and let them make it to the negative when it suits the alienator. The children will most likely be lead to feel that you are not deserving of their love and affection because you treat them badly, anything that you may do or say apart from being perfect may be used against you in this way.

Your family and friends ... in most cases the alienator will attempt to discredit them also ... "his/her brother, your uncle, is a fat alcoholic drug using nobody" ... now if this is true there may be some fair basis but by now it is true in the children's minds, especially if the uncle is fat, and whilst the alienator has not targeted you directly they have discredited you, by association. The alienator uses some fact to strengthen a lie and all the children see is the fact that the uncle is fat so the rest must be true. Discredit enough of your friends and family and you are discredited in the eyes of the children.

Home is where the heart is ... and rightfully so but the alienator takes every opportunity to drive this home and that their heart really belongs at the alienators place ... "are you happier here or over there" ... the children do not want to disappoint so they say here and if gone over enough it becomes reality, it is a lot easier for them that way and the end result is that they do not feel at home at the the other parents place hence no or little love or sense of belonging at the home of the targeted, end result is that they do not want to be there.

"If you loved us you would just want us to be happy" ... and by now guess where they think (coached) they are the happiest ... "if you loved us you would just want us to be happy and you would not care what the judge said, you would let us go" ... this is a very difficult one as by the time they have got up the courage to say it (coached) then they really think it and then you become the baddy by not letting them go. The alienator knows you won't so again you loose.

Holidays ... do not tell the children where you plan to take them on holidays, if you do they will most likely tell the alienator giving the alienator an opportunity to discredit the event by pointing out the dangers etc ... camping, "be carefull of all the snakes and spiders" ... in the end the children are not keen to go and the excitement of it all is gone, you have made the bookings and they do not want to go but you go and they are angry with you even after they have settled down and ultimately enjoy the holiday ... "it is dangerous to take children camping in the bush" leaves the children thinking you are willing to put them in danger, not a good parent.

This site was prepared and is run by private individuals who have felt the pain ... there is no commercial affiliation of any type whatsoever.

The end of a romantic relationship is always difficult for parents. It can be just as difficult, if not worse, for their children. How children deal with the end of their parents' relationship has to do with two things: the age and maturity of the children, and how their parents manage the breakdown of their relationship.

Children don't see things in terms of "custody" or "parental responsibilities" when their parents' relationship ends. All they know is that something has gone wrong. Mom and dad are yelling at each other a lot, and then, one day, mom or dad isn't there anymore. Young children won't understand these adult problems. Children who are in primary school will have a better idea, since they'll have friends whose parents have separated. Pre-teens and teens may seem to have a much more grown-up grasp of things as they'll have lost relationships of their own, and may be able to appreciate the idea that their parents' relationship has ended. How children cope with their parents' separation changes as they grow older and more mature.

Things are a lot different for parents. A significant relationship has ended, and in the midst of all of the emotions that go along with that — grief, anger, jealousy, love and loss — they might find themselves also having to deal with some extremely difficult legal issues. It's even worse where the parents wind up fighting about things in court.

Litigation can have a very profound impact on people. At its core, litigation is an adversarial process: each parent is fighting the other in order to "win," and where there's a winner there's always a loser. This sort of approach to a dispute often polarizes parents and encourages them to take extreme positions. What makes this so much worse is that the parents are both fighting about something they cherish dearly, their children, and they are both fighting against someone whom they used to deeply love.

In circumstances like these, it can be easy to forget how important it is that the children maintain a positive, loving relationship with the other parent. It can also be easy to overlook the importance of managing the children's exposure to and perception of their parents' conflict. One parent's view of the other becomes clouded by hatred, malice and spite, and nothing the other parent can do is ever right. This attitude is almost impossible to shield from the children. Whether intentionally or unintentionally, the children are inevitably exposed to these negative views which, without interference, can come to colour the children's own views of the other parent.

Children's experiences of separation

It is important to remember that while one parent's thoughtless comments about the other parent can have an impact on how a child sees the other parent, so too will the child's own experience of the separation. This can include:

blaming the parent who left for breaking up the family,

seeing a parent as injured by the actions of the other parent,

sympathizing with an emotionally upset parent, and

missing and feeling sad for the parent that they see less often.

These feelings may have nothing at all to do with any blameworthy conduct on the part of either parent, but they can cause a child to feel closer to one parent than the other. Further, there a number of normal reasons why a child might feel closer to one parent even in families that haven't separated, such as:

similarities in the temperament of the child and one of the parents,the parent's gender,interests the child shares with a parent, and how the parent handles discipline.

There are, of course, ways that parents can behave, intentionally and unintentionally, that will encourage a child to drift towards one parent and away from the other that are blameworthy. Remember, however, that there are normal reasons why a child's experience of divorce may align with one parent over the other that have nothing to do with a parent's conduct.

Resisting visits with a parent

When a child begins to drift apart from a parent, the first sign that this might become a serious problem often occurs when the child begins to express a reluctance to spend time with the other parent. It is important to distinguish a simple reluctance from a more serious problem like estrangement or alienation. It is also important to distinguish between a reluctance that stems from a child and a reluctance that is fostered by a parent. In a sense, this is the key difference between estrangement and alienation.

Normal reasons why a child might resist parenting time or contact include age-appropriate separation anxieties,

inability to cope with the transition between homes, especially where there is a lot of conflict between the parents,

not wanting to leave an upset parent at home, and

not liking the other parent's parenting style.

Of course, any resistance to separation is difficult for both parents. For the parent sending the child on the visit, it can be heart wrenching to force the child out the door. For the parent receiving the child, it can be devastating to hear — from the other parent or the child — that the parenting time or contact is unwelcome, and to experience the rejection that this entails.

These "normal" reasons why a child would be reluctant to see a parent can be aggravated by the unintentional conduct of each parent. Separated parents have a positive duty to nurture their child's relationship with the other parent. In the context of parenting time and contact, this means encouraging the child to look forward to seeing the other parent. In general, this means actively fostering the child's relationship with the other parent and refraining from making negative remarks about the other parent.

In high-conflict situations, even parents who understand this basic duty can unconsciously telegraph their feelings about the other parent to the child. Children are not stupid; they know something's not right. Even young children will pick up on non-verbal clues to a parent's feelings.

This sort of unintentional communication of emotion includes:

making faces, grimacing, groaning, cringing or shuddering when the other parent is mentioned,

arguing with the other parent when the children can see or hear the dispute,

making negative comments about the other parent when the children are within earshot, using an emotionless or negative tone of voice when speaking to the children about the other parent, and

reacting in a flat or negative manner when the children discuss the other parent or their activities with that parent.

Even though in these examples nothing is actually being said to the children to discourage their relationship with the other parent, they will pick up on the implications these behaviours suggest: there is something bad about one parent which is hurting the other parent. This sort of behaviour will inevitably encourage and reinforce any resistance the child might have to seeing the other parent.

When a child begins to express a reluctance to visit the other parent, both parents must act to stop the problem from getting worse.

For the parent who has the child most often, this means that you must:

work harder at encouraging the child to look forward to the visits,

make sure that you are not a part of the problem by unconsciously telegraphing your problems with the other parent,

make an effort to remind the child about the other parent's positive traits,

consider getting the child in to see a counsellor about the separation, and

seriously consider taking a parenting after separation course.

For the parent whom the child is resisting seeing, this means that you must:

work harder at making the child feel welcomed and listened to in your home,

re-examine your approach to parenting issues, particularly if you were the disciplinarian during your relationship with the other parent,

make sure that you are not insulting or mocking the other parent when the child is within earshot, and

seriously consider taking a parenting after separation course.

None of these solutions may be effective if the child's opinion and emotions are too entrenched, if the parents are simply too angry with one another to cooperate effectively, or if one of the parents is actively working to undermine the other parent's relationship with the child.

When things go too far, or when a problem is left unchecked, a child's simple preference for one parent can develop to an extreme point, where the child is estranged or alienated from the other parent.

Knowing when there's a problem

An otherwise "normal" resistance to parenting time or contact can cross the line when the child's opinion of the parent and his or her emotional attachment to that parent begins to change. Temper tantrums about a visit, and expressions of rage and hate should send a loud and clear signal that both parents have to work a lot harder to help the child through his or her experience of the separation.

Mild expressions of a change in the child's attachment to a parent include:

Expressing ambivalence about visiting the parent (not caring one way or the other about seeing the parent).

Grumbling about having to go to see the other parent.

Stating a preference for an activity (playing a game, seeing friends and so forth) over seeing the other parent.

More serious expressions of a change in the child's attachment to a parent include:

Expressing a preference for one parent over the other, and a general ambivalence about the other parent.

Expressing a preference for one home over the other.

Expressing a worry about missing the parent the child is leaving.

Being upset that an activity (playing a game, an outing, seeing friends and so forth) will be interrupted by the visit.

Stating that visits with other parent are boring.

Being reluctant to speak to the other parent on the telephone.

Still more serious expressions of a change include

Stating that he or she "doesn't like" the other parent.

Occasionally putting the other parent down.

Expressions of concern for the well-being of the parent the child is leaving for the visit (older children).

Crying before the visit (younger children).

Complaining that "it's not fair" to have to visit (older children).

Don't believe what they say: that Parental Alienation cannot happen to older children, that it's just an oxymoron.

Parental Alienation is the act of one parent deliberately undermining the relationship between the children and the other parent to the point of creating a hostile relationship and thus alienation of the children from the other parent. Another way to look at this is alienation of affection, which is one of the basic human needs discussed at length by Maslow in his Hierarchy of Needs. It is a

serious form of psychological abuse, and it is very dangerous because it occurs internally and, thus, is harder to treat. Unlike physical abuse where the scars and wounds are on the outside, Parental Alienation Syndrome (PAS) is so deep inside that unlocking the key to it takes years of treatment and unconditional love.

Though PAS is primarily seen in high-conflict divorces, it also occurs in intact families. And though it usually begins in early childhood, this is not always the case, and does not mean that older children and even adults cannot be alienated from their other parent. In fact, PAS is often described as a cult form of control over others. In this respect, we can say that the perpetrator or

alienator brainwashes and programs the innocent victims to hate their other parent/family members. In much the way as the leaders of cults, like Jonestown, these perpetrators are able to take a person and convert him or her into the alienator's way of thinking and to renounce all ties with the victim's families and friends. If a cult leader can do this to total strangers who have no familial ties to them, then it is safe to say that it would be that much easier for a parent to do this to his or her children, no matter what age they are.

Parents and family have a much stronger bind or hold upon children. In fact, a child, no matter what age, would be more likely to listen to and believe his or her parent than a total stranger. Therefore, any judge, counselor, agency or attorney claiming that an older child could not be alienated from his or her other parent, is actually stating that cults, like the Branch Davidians, could not possibly happen. In these non-believers' minds, only children can be brainwashed and programmed. This defies logic, as it is a proven fact that cults do brainwash people and program them, and most of these cult followers are adults. In other words, if a total stranger can turn a person against his or her family, then a parent can do it even more easily, no matter the age of the child.

Furthermore, as Amy J. L. Baker points out in her book, Adult Children of Parental Alienation Syndrome – Breaking the Ties that Bind, adolescents are just as vulnerable to the tactics used to impede a relationship with the other parent. These young adults are at a point in their lives where they are allowed more responsibility to make their own decisions, and one of those is custody and visitation. Baker feels that alienators are probably quite aware of this and utilize this idea as they intensify their tactics to distance the children from the other parent. In addition to this issue, young adults are struggling for their independence from their parents and if one parent, the alienator, offers them more freedom and thus are more liberal with them, the children will be swayed easily to side with this parent. Alienators know this very well, and actually use this same technique when bribing their children monetarily with gifts and toys. (Baker, p. 182-183) Alienators are good exploiters of weaknesses in people. They will go after the weakest link to break the chain and command control of the other links in the chain. What better way to do this than with bribery and offerings.

Case in point: two children who are raised since birth to hate their father's side of his family. The children are repeatedly told that relatives from their father's side of the family are no good and crazy and that the children are never to spend time alone with them. Their mother even tries to convince their father that his side of the family is not good and actually rarely lets the kids visit their paternal grandparents, niece, or nephew. Fast-forward 15 years, to a failed marriage. Though the children have spent very positive and rewarding times with their father and his family especially during the holiday seasons, in the back of their minds, they have been programmed to not trust them. So when the father initiates a divorce, instantly the mother begins to denigrate and berate the father. The children, though 14 and 16, are easily turned against their father and refuse to spend time with him, and when they do, they are disrespectful and rude. Despite the judge's orders, these two teenagers are too enmeshed with their mother's hatred, anger, and faulty beliefs that their relationship with their father is near non-existent. Despite 15 years of positive good memories that they could draw upon, the years of programming and brainwashing have taken their toll.PAS does not differentiate age. PAS does not prejudice only the very young. PAS is real and can affect anyone of any age and gender. It is ageless, genderless and most of all, the most painful form of psychological abuse a guardian can inflict on another human being. Until the judges, counsellors, agencies and attorneys accept the fact that PAS has no preferences and can occur to anyone at any time in his or her life, this form of Domestic Violence will continue to grow and destroy families

There is an old African proverb that states "when two elephants fight it is the grass under their feet that suffers". Similarly, when parents fight over custody and access of their children after a separation it is the children that suffer. In many cases the parents are not even aware of the effect that their custody battle is having on their children and they do not intend to hurt their children. Nevertheless, research shows that children who have lived through a high conflict divorce have a greater tendency to develop mental health issues, addiction issues, are less likely to obtain a post-secondary education and have a whole host of other social problems that develop later on in their lives as a result of their negative experience.

In some of the more extreme high conflict custody cases, a dynamic develops whereby one of the parents sets out to sever the children's ties to the other parent. The American psychiatrist who first coined the phrase "parental alienation" described it as, "a disorder that arises primarily in the context of child custody disputes. Its primary manifestation is the child's campaign of denigration against a parent, a campaign that has no justification. It results from the combination of a programming parent's indoctrinations and the child's own contributions to the vilification of the target parent."Some of the symptoms of Parental Alienation Syndrome (PAS) which will be added as a diagnosis under the DSM in 2010, are as follows

The alienated child:

- Sees one parent as all good and other parent as all bad; parents

As with most things in life, there is a wide spectrum of severity and the blame usually does not fall on one person's shoulders only. The "alienated parent" often contributes to the problem by making the child feel guilty, rejecting the child, acting aggressively towards the child or to the other parent or by simply giving up hope and abandoning the child. Also, some children are estranged from a parent prior to the separation and it only gets worse after wards. The alienating parents often act the way they do because they feel that they have been abandoned by the other parent and are very hurt by the separation. They themselves may have been abandoned or abused as children.

Richard Gardner and some of his followers are of the view that the only cure to this problem is to take the child out of the custody of the alienating parent, subject the child to intense counseling to de-brainwash the child and then place the child in the alienated parent's custody.

Not surprisingly, there are many family court judges who do not accept that this is the only solution to the problem. Instead, they try to affect a change in the dynamic by making access orders enforceable by the police, making a parent who is withholding access pay a fine or even ordering that the alienating parent go to jail if they breach the access order again.

In the US there are some residential programs available for families with this problem. In Canada, there are therapists who specialize in assisting families with this problem, but there are no residential programs that I am aware of.

In my view the essential thing is to prevent the alienation from happening in the first place. This can be done by identifying the early symptoms and ensuring that there is an access plan in place very shortly after the separation that is strongly enforced by the court. It is also essential that all parties involved get counseling to identify the issues that are at the root of the problem and bring them to the surface and that professionals involved in helping parents who are separating and divorcing are trained to recognize the early symptoms.

There have been recent amendments made to the Children's Law Reform Act to reinforce the idea that maximum contact with both parents is generally in the best interests of children and that parents have an obligation not only to allow access, but to facilitate that access.

If you are fearful that this dynamic may be occurring in your family, please don't wait for things to get better. Parental alienation is like cancer- if left untreated it will grow and kill your relationship with your child. Children in families where there is this dynamic are "victims" of abuse and end up exhibiting the same symptoms as children who are physically and sexually abused by their family members. You have a responsibility to protect your children from this abuse, as do all the professionals who are involved in your case.

Parental alienation syndrome (PAS) and parental alienation (PA) are often invoked in legal and legislative contexts addressing the rights of fathers and mothers in custody or visitation litigation. Indeed, alienation claims have become ubiquitous in custody cases where domestic violence or child abuse is alleged, as grounds to reject mothers' requests to limit paternal access to their children. This paper provides a historical and research overview of PAS and PA, identifies strategic issues for advocates working with abused women and children,* and offers guidelines to improve courts' treatment of these issues. While PAS and PA have much in common both as theories and with respect to how they are used in court, they have distinct scientific and research bases and critiques. This paper, therefore, addresses them separately.

Parental Alienation Syndrome

Historical Background

The notion of children's hostility to one parent in the context of divorce was first characterized as a pathology by divorce researchers Wallerstein and Kelly. They theorized that a child's rejection of a noncustodial parent and strong resistance or refusal to visit that parent was sometimes a "pathological" alignment between an angry custodial parent and an older child or adolescent and that this alliance was fueled by the dynamics of marital separation, including a child's reaction to it (Wallerstein & Kelly, 1976, 1980). Although significant, Wallerstein and Kelly's construct did not become a staple of custody evaluations or judicial determinations. Moreover, their early work does not use the phrase "parental alienation," but focuses instead on children's "alignment" with one parent against the other.

Beginning in the early 1980's, attention to a purported "parental alienation syndrome" exploded as the result of the dedicated efforts of Richard Gardner, a psychiatrist loosely affiliated with Columbia Medical School1 who ran a clinical practice that focused on counselling divorcing parents.

Based solely on his interpretation of data gathered from his clinical practice, Gardner posited that child sexual abuse allegations were rampant in custody litigation, and that 90% of children in custody litigation suffered from a disorder, which he called "Parental Alienation Syndrome (PAS)." He described PAS as a "syndrome" whereby vengeful mothers employed child abuse allegations as a powerful weapon to punish ex-husbands and ensure custody to themselves (Gardner, 1992a; 1992b). He further theorized that such mothers enlisted the children in their "campaign of denigration" and "vilification" of the father, that they often "brainwashed" or "programmed" the children into believing untrue claims of abuse by the father, and that the children then fabricated and contributed their own stories (Gardner, 1992b, p. 162, 193; 2002, pp. 94-95). He claimed – based solely on his own interpretation of his own clinical experience – that the majority of child sexual abuse claims in custody litigation are false (Gardner, 1991), although he suggested that some mothers' vendettas were the product of pathology rather than intentional malice (Gardner, 1987, 1992b). In short, Gardner claimed that when children reject their father and they or their mother makes abuse allegations, this behavior is most likely the product of PAS rather than actual experiences of abuse. PAS theory is thus premised on the assumption that child abuse claimants' believability and trustworthiness is highly suspect.2

While acknowledging that if there was actually abuse which explained a child's hostility there could be no PAS (Gardner, 1992a), Gardner's "diagnostic criteria" focused on various personality characteristics of the accuser, accused, and the child, rather than expert assessments of abuse itself or the other reasons that might explain a child's hostility to a parent (Gardner, 1992b; see also Hoult, 2006). Rather, Gardner's PAS theory presumes that a child's hostility to a father is pathological, which, in turn, encourages courts to suspect that mothers who make such allegations are doing so only to undermine the child's relationship with the father. Indeed, in differentiating between "fabricated" and "bona fide" abuse, Gardner uses "the Presence of the Parental Alienation Syndrome" as itself an "extremely valuable differentiating [criterion]" (Gardner, 1987, p. 109). By PAS, as previously discussed, he means a child's "campaign of denigration" of the father and the mother's supposed "programming" of the child/ren (Gardner, 2002, pp. 95-97). In short, Gardner's PAS theory essentially presumes PAS's existence from the mere presence of a child's hostility toward and/or fear of their father based on alleged abuse. This is unfortunately precisely how it has been applied in many courts.

It should be further noted that the "Sexual Abuse Legitimacy Scale," which Gardner invented as a means of quantifying the likelihood that sexual abuse claims were valid, was so excoriated by scientific experts as "garbage" that he withdrew the scale; however, many of the factors it contained continue to be part of his qualitative discussions of how to determine whether child sexual abuse allegations are legitimate (Bruch, 2001; Faller, 1998).

Gardner's Remedies for PAS

Gardner's "remedy" for purportedly severe PAS is extreme - including complete denial of maternal-child contact and "de-programming" the child through a concerted brainwashing effort to change the child's beliefs that they have been abused (Bruch, 2001; Gardner, 1992a; see also www.rachelfoundation.org). After being subjected to these procedures and ordered by the court to live with the father they said abused them, some children became suicidal and some killed themselves (Bruch, 2001; Hoult, 2006). In other cases, courts have ordered children into jail and juvenile homes as part of Gardner's recommended "threat therapy" which is the stock in trade of strict alienation psychologists (Hoult, 2006; Johnston & Kelly, 2004a). In one such case, a judge ordered a frail nine-year-old boy seized by three police officers and placed in a juvenile detention facility when he refused to get into his father's car for a scheduled visitation. The son of the father's girlfriend had sexually abused the boy, and he had also witnessed the father's violence against his mother. After three days of abuse by the other boys in the detention facility, the boy agreed to cooperate with the court order. The judge concluded that his "treatment" for parental alienation had worked (E. Stark, personal communication, May 2007).

As critiques of PAS have pointed out, PAS is a teflon defense to an accusation of abuse, because all evidence brought to bear to support the abuse claims is simply reframed as further evidence of the "syndrome" (Bruch, 2001). That is, all efforts to gather corroboration of the allegations are simply treated as further evidence of her pathological need to "alienate" the child from the father (Gardner, 1987, 1992a). If the protective parent points to a therapist's opinion that the child has been abused, the therapist is accused of a "folie a trois" (a clinical term from the French for "folly of three") which suggests that all three parties are in a dysfunctional "dance" together (Bruch, 2001). A child's or a protective parent's repetition of claims of abuse is routinely characterized as further evidence of extreme alienation, and punished by court orders prohibiting continued reporting of abuse.

Gardner's pro-pedophilic and misogynistic beliefs

Gardner's underlying beliefs regarding human sexuality, including adult-child sexual interaction, are so extreme and unfounded that it is hard to believe that courts would have adopted his theory had they known. First, he asserted that the reason women lie about child sexual abuse in custody litigation is because "hell hath no fury like a woman scorned" (Gardner, 1992b, pp. 218-19), and/or because they are "gratifie[d] vicariously" (Gardner, 1991, p. 25; 1992a, p. 126) by imagining their child having sex with the father. There is of course no empirical basis or support for these offensive assertions.

Second, Gardner's views of sexuality were disturbing. He claimed that all human sexual paraphilias, including pedophilia, sadism, rape, necrophilia, zoophilia (sex with animals), coprophilia (sex with feces), and other deviant behaviors "serve the purposes of species survival" by "enhanc[ing] the general level of sexual excitation in society" (Gardner, 1992b, p. 20; see also Hoult, 2006; Dallam, 1998.)

Further, Gardner claimed that women's physiology and conditioning makes them potentially masochistic rape victims who may "gain pleasure from being beaten, bound, and otherwise made to suffer," as "the price they are willing to pay for gaining the gratification of receiving the sperm" (Gardner, 1992b, p. 26).

Regarding pedophilia, Gardner argued expressly that adult-child sex need not be intrinsically harmful to children, and that it is beneficial to the species, insofar as it increases a child's sexualization and increases the likelihood that his or her genes will be transmitted at an early age (Gardner, 1992b). Gardner claimed, "sexual activities between an adult and a child are an ancient tradition" and phenomenon which "has been present in just about every society studied, both past and present" (Gardner, 1992b, pp. 47-48). He viewed Western society as "excessively punitive" in its treatment of pedophilia as a "sickness and a crime" (Gardner, 1991, p. 115), and attributed this "overreaction" to the influence of the Jews (Gardner, 1992b, pp. 47, 49). Gardner opposed mandated reporting of child sexual abuse and specifically described a case in which he successfully persuaded a mother not to report a bus driver who had molested her daughter, because it would "interfere with the natural desensitization process, would be likely to enhance guilt, and would have other untoward psychological effects" (Gardner, 1992b, pp. 611-12; see also Dallam, 1998). Gardner's perspective on adult-child sexual interaction can be summed up in his reference to Shakespeare's famous quote: "'There is nothing either good or bad, but thinking makes it so'" (Gardner, 1991, p. 115).

Despite his assertions that paedophilia is widespread and harmless, he asserted in a filmed interview that a child who tells his mother he has been sexually molested by his or her father should be told "I don't believe you. I'm going to beat you for saying it. Don't you ever talk that way again about your father" (Waller, 2001).3 This response – and his beliefs described above – suggest that the animating intention behind the PAS theory's denial of the validity of child sexual abuse reports is not a genuine belief that child sexual abuse is often falsely reported, but rather a belief that such reports should be suppressed.

While Gardner and PAS have had many adherents, particularly among forensic evaluators and litigants, there is actually no empirical research validating the existence of PAS. And there is extensive empirical proof that the assumptions underlying the theory are false.

Sole empirical study of PAS does not validate the concept. Only one study has been published that purports to empirically verify the existence of PAS. Consistent with scientific standards, this study sought to assess the "inter-rater reliability" of PAS – i.e., the extent to which different observers can consistently identify PAS (Rueda, 2004). The study built directly on Gardner's criteria, taking for granted that those criteria reflect PAS. It then measured the degree to which a small sample of therapists agreed on whether five case scenarios presented to them reflect those PAS criteria or not (Rueda, 2004). The findings were that there was a reasonable degree of agreement about whether these cases indicated PAS. However, the findings do not prove its existence – rather, they prove that a small number of mental health professionals agreed on applying the label PAS to cases of estranged ("alienated") children. Many therapists surveyed, however, had refused to fill out the questionnaire and some expressly stated they didn't believe PAS existed. This study thus simply presumed rather than proved the key question: is the concept of PAS actually a disorder caused by a malevolent aligned parent's efforts, or is it simply a reframing of a child's estrangement flowing from abuse, other problematic conduct by the alienated parent, or other normative reasons? The author himself admits that the findings did not "differentiate PAS from parental alienation" (Rueda, 2004, p. 400). Since "parental alienation" is merely a label that does not in itself explain the reason for the child's alienation, this admission essentially negates the study as a validator of PAS. PAS' empirical bases are false or unsupported. The claims upon which Gardner based his PAS theory are thoroughly contradicted by the empirical research. First, Gardner (1991, 1992b) claimed that child sexual abuse allegations are widespread in custody cases and that the vast majority of such allegations are false. These claims have no empirical basis, other than Gardner's interpretation of his own clinical practice. In contradiction, the largest study of child sexual abuse allegations in custody litigation ever conducted found that child sexual abuse allegations were extremely rare (less than 2% of cases) and of those, approximately 50% of the claims were deemed valid, even when assessed by normally conservative court and agency evaluators (Thoennes & Tjaden, 1990). Other studies have found such allegations to be validated approximately 70% of the time (Faller, 1998). Moreover, leading researchers have found that the dominant problem in child sexual abuse evaluation is not false allegations, but rather, the "high rates of unsubstantiated maltreatment" in "circumstances that indicat[e] that abuse or neglect may have occurred" (Trocme & Bala, 2005, pp. 1342-44).

Indeed, empirical research has found that the PAS theory is built upon an assumption which is the opposite of the truth: Where PAS presumes that protective mothers are vengeful and pathologically "program" their children, it is not women and children – but noncustodial fathers – who are most likely to fabricate child maltreatment claims. In the largest study of its kind, leading researchers analyzed the 1998 Canadian Incidence Study of Reported Child Abuse and Neglect. They found that only 12% of child abuse or neglect allegations made in the context of litigation over child access were intentionally false (Trocme & Bala, 2005). Notably, they found that the primary source (43%) of these intentionally false reports was noncustodial parents (typically fathers); relatives, neighbors, or acquaintances accounted for another 19% of false reports. Only 14% of knowingly false claims were made by custodial parents (typically mothers), and only two cases (out of 308) fit the alienation paradigm of an intentionally false abuse allegations against a noncustodial father (Trocme & Bala, 2005).

PAS has been rejected as invalid by scientific and professional authorities. The dominant consensus in the scientific community is that there is no scientific evidence of a clinical "syndrome" concerning "parental alienation." Leading researchers, including some who treat "alienation" itself as a real problem, concur, "The scientific status of PAS is, to be blunt, nil" (Emery, Otto, & O'Donohue, 2005, p. 10; see also Gould, 2006; Johnston & Kelly, 2004b; Myers, Berliner, Briere, Hendrix, Jenny, and Reid, 2002; Smith and Coukos, 1997; Wood, 1994). The Presidential Task Force of the American Psychological Association on Violence in the Family stated as early as 1996 that "[a]lthough there are no data to support the phenomenon called parental alienation syndrome, in which mothers are blamed for interfering with their children's attachment to their fathers, the term is still used by some evaluators and Courts to discount children's fears in hostile and psychologically abusive situations" (p. 40). Dr. Paul Fink, past President of the American Psychiatric Association, describes PAS as "junk science" (Talan, 2003, line 9). Nonetheless, defenses of PAS against critiques have led even some respected social scientists to mis-cite and distort the research (Lasseur & Meier, 2005).

Thus, PAS has been rejected multiple times by the American Psychiatric Association as lacking in scientific basis and therefore not worthy of inclusion in the Diagnostic and Statistical Manual of Mental Disorders. The most recent all-out campaign by PAS proponents for inclusion of (the re-named) "Parental Alienation Disorder" (PAD) was flatly rejected by the DSM-V committee in 2012 (Crary, 2012).

Echoing the scientific consensus, a leading judicial body, the National Council of Juvenile and Family Court Judges (NCJFCJ), has published guidelines for custody courts stating:

[t]he discredited "diagnosis" of "PAS" (or allegation of "parental alienation"), quite apart from its scientific invalidity, inappropriately asks the court to assume that the children's behaviors and attitudes toward the parent who claims to be "alienated" have no grounding in reality. It also diverts attention away from the

behaviors of the abusive parent, who may have directly influenced the children's responses by acting in violent, disrespectful, intimidating, humiliating and/or discrediting ways toward the children themselves, or the children's other parent

In contrast to PAS theory that views the indoctrinating parent as the principal player in the child's alienation, this study [their own] found that children's rejection of a parent had multiple determinants . . . [another study of theirs also] supported a multi-dimensional explanation of children's rejection of a parent, with both parents as well as vulnerabilities within the child contributing to the problem. Alienating behavior by an emotionally needy aligned parent (mother or father), with whom the child was in role-reversal, were strong predictors of the child's rejection of the other parent. Just as important as contributors were critical incidents of child abuse and/or lack of warm, involved parenting by the rejected parent (pp. 80-81).

Johnston also differentiates her approach from Gardner's by rejecting his draconian "remedies," including custody switching to the "hated" parent. Characterizing Gardner's prescriptions as "a license for tyranny," Johnston and Kelly (2004b, p. 85) call instead for individualized assessments of both the children and the parents' parenting, maintaining focus on the children's needs rather than the parents' rights. In theory, the goal is a more realistic and healthy relationship with both parents, rather than reconciliation with the hated parent as the only desirable goal (Johnston, 2005). Unfortunately, the common practice in court is far less nuanced and individualized (see below).

The notion that some children are alienated from a parent is both a less scientific and more factual assertion. It is thus easier to raise "alienation" in court without triggering a battle over the admissibility of scientific evidence (Gardner, 2002). However, debate continues to rage in research and advocacy circles over the extent to which parental alienation is something that can be measured, is caused by a parent, and/or has truly harmful effects, or whether it is simply a new less objectionable name for the invalidated PAS. To the extent that PA is widely used almost identically to PAS in court, it may not matter in practice what the theoretical differences are.

Critique of PA - Lack of Evidence Base

Questioning the scientific basis of parental alienation and PAS is challenging because these theories are described and referenced in a substantial social science literature. Many of these materials make assertions about PAS and PA without any citation to scientific literature – yet their "publication" on the Internet and their association with apparently credentialed authors and/or supporters, give them an aura of credibility. Some articles do cite research selectively, but contain numerous unsupported assertions as well, about PAS, PA, and how they operate.

Custody evaluators and psychologists frequently insist as an anecdotal matter that alienation is present and is a terrible thing. However, the only existing empirical basis for this assumption of alienation's harmfulness at this time is limited to "clinical observation" (Johnston & Kelly, 2004b; see also Ackerman & Dolezal, 2006). Of course clinical observations are subjective, and do not constitute empirical evidence. Moreover, these statements do not indicate whether the relationship breaches between children and parents observed by these clinicians are a healthy or developmental response to their relationship with that parent, or if the "alienation" is wrongfully instigated by a favoured ("aligned") parent (Johnston & Kelly, 2004b). Indeed, even if the clinical observers attempted to make the distinction, there would be no objective way of discerning whether their judgment was correct (short of a comprehensive assessment of the child-parent relationship, including any abusive, neglectful or cold, indifferent or hostile parenting by the disliked parent.

In fact, what the empirical evidence Johnston et al. (2005) have amassed indicates both that (i) actual "alienation" of a child is quite rare despite many parents' derogatory conduct or statements about the other parent and (ii) when children are estranged from a parent there are always multiple reasons, some of which are that parent's own conduct. Their widely published research has found that, despite the alienating behaviors of both parents in most of the families participating in their study, only 20% of children were actually "alienated" and only 6% were "severely alienated." Even among the children who rejected a parent, all had multiple reasons for their hostility, including negative behaviors by the hated parent, such as child abuse or inadequate parenting, or the children's own developmental or personality difficulties (Johnston, 2005; Johnston et al., 2005).

The fact that only a small fraction of children subjected to inter-parental hostilities and alienating conduct by their parents have been found to actually become "alienated" suggests that the focus on alienation is a tempest in a teapot – one that continues to distract from and undermine the accurate assessment of abuse and concomitant risks to children.

Lack of Evidence Base for Long-term Impact of Alienation

Johnston and others have acknowledged that "there is very little empirical data to back up their "clinical observations" that alienated children are significantly undermined in their emotional and psychological development. In fact, Johnston and Kelly (2004b) forthrightly state that "there are no systematic long-term data on the adjustment and well-being of alienated compared to non-alienated children so that long-term prognostications are merely speculative" (p. 84). And, contrary to the common assertions of evaluators and alienation theorists that alienation is a devastating form of emotional abuse of children, Judith Wallerstein, the groundbreaking researcher of divorce who first pointed out the problem of children's sometimes pathological alignment with the custodial parent after divorce, found in her follow-up study that children's hostility toward the other parent after divorce was in every case temporary, and resolved of its own accord, mostly within one or two years (Bruch, 2001; Wallerstein et al., 2000).

Perhaps the most disturbing misuse of PA is seen when PA adherents fail to distinguish between children who are estranged from a non-custodial parent due to abuse or other negative behavior from children who have been wrongly influenced by their favored parent to hate or fear the other. Thus, leading adherents to PA theory including Johnston and colleagues sometimes describe children's symptoms and psychological harms and attribute them to "alienation," while simultaneously acknowledging that their research shows that "alienated" children include those who are justifiably estranged due to the disfavored parent's conduct. Cases worked on by this author have shown that abused children display many of the symptoms that are frequently attributed to "alienation" both in the courts and in this literature (Compare Johnston, Walters, & Olesen, 2005; Johnston & Kelly, 2004b with Kathleen C. Faller, 1999; Righthand, 2003). Such discussions attribute to alienation harms which, in fact, may well be due to the disfavored parent's own behaviors (Meier, 2010).

This failure to distinguish between whether harm to children – or their hostility to their father – is caused by alienation or abuse sets up a paradoxically disastrous dynamic: So long as an abuser can convince a court that the children's attitudes can be labelled "alienation," he can benefit from the very impact of his abuse. In Jordan v. Jordan, the trial court found (based on two alienation psychologists' testimony) that the older of two children was severely alienated from her father, who had been found to have twice committed interfamily offenses against the mother. Therefore, the court ruled that the legislative presumption against joint custody to a batterer was rebutted – by the child's alienation, which, the court stated, would cause her emotional damage, and which it was presumed could best be cured by more time with her father (who she adamantly refused to see). The problem with this analysis was that neither the experts nor the judge considered the possibility that the child's "alienation" may have been at least in part a reaction to the father's violence toward the mother and in front of the child, as well as his known manhandling of the child herself. As a result, the father won joint (and eventually, sole) custody, even though the possibility that the child's hostility was a function of his own abusive behaviours was never ruled out (Jordan, 2010). When this argument was put before the Court of Appeals, that Court also ignored the fact that such reasoning makes battering a sure path to an award of custody – so long as the children become alienated as a result. The Court simply affirmed that the alienation label is sufficient grounds to rebut the presumption against custody to batterers, without regard to whether it is the batterer's own abuse which may have caused the child's "alienation" (Jordan, 2011).

It should be noted that, while alienation researchers do not discuss child witnessing of adult domestic violence as a form of emotional child abuse, research has unequivocally found that child witnesses to adult abuse can be profoundly negatively affected and/or traumatized, even if they are not themselves the direct target of physical or sexual violence (Lewis-O'Connor, Sharps, Humphreys, Gary, & Campbell, 2006; Bancroft & Silverman, 2012). Therefore, even where children have not been directly abused themselves, their fear or hostility toward the batterer of their mother may be entirely expected.

The fact that courts are not nuanced in applying alienation theory would not in itself be sufficient to indict the theory itself. However, discussions of PA within the scholarly literature supporting the concept demonstrate that these applications of the theory are quite consistent with the way it is understood by its researchers and theorists. For instance, while on the one hand conveying a more reasonable awareness of the many factors that contribute to a child's alienation from a parent, Johnston and collaborators continue to pathologies mothers whose children are hostile or afraid of their fathers. In some of their earlier work they even go so far as to pathologies the "aligned" parent who "often fervently believes that the rejected parent is dangerous to the child in some way(s): violent, physically or sexually abusive, or neglectful" (p. 258). They go on to describe the pursuit of legal protections and other means of assuring safety as a "campaign to protect the child from the presumed danger [which] is mounted on multiple fronts [including] restraining orders…" (p. 258). Finally, like Gardner, these purported rejectors of PAS continue to assert that a parent can "unconsciously" denigrate the other parent to the child "as a consequence of their own deep psychological issues" which cause them to "harbor deep distrust and fear of the ex-spouse…" (p. 257; see also Meier, 2010). This willingness to pathologize capable mothers even extends to mothers' "warm, involved" parenting – which they assert can powerfully fuel alienation in a child (Johnston et al., 2005, p. 208; Kelly and Johnston, 2001). Such discussions are more than sufficient to ensure that whenever a mother and child have ambivalence about the children's father, and certainly in most cases where mothers allege abuse, virtually any loving parenting by the mother can be labeled a form of "alienation."

In short, parental alienation as a theory has been built – not by scientific or empirical research, but by repeated assertions – at first more extreme assertions by Gardner, and now less extreme but still distorted assertions by more sophisticated psychological professionals. Unfortunately it has been used virtually identically to PAS in family courts, to simply turn abuse allegations back against the protective parent and children (Meier, 2010). Anecdotal experience is now being confirmed by cutting edge research into "turned around" cases, i.e., those in which a court initially disbelieves a father is dangerous and, after some harm to the children, a second court corrects the error. Preliminary results of this research have identified PA labelling as one of three primary factors leading to erroneous denials of an accused abuser (usually a father)'s dangerousness, and orders subjecting children to on-going abuse. These preliminary results indicate that at least 37% of initial case errors of 10 out of 27 were attributable to PA/PAS labelling. If an additional 12 cases in which the protective parent usually a mother was pathologies in similar manner without the PA labellng are included, the percentage becomes 66%. Opinions of evaluators and Guardians of both were key factor in the court's unproductive erroneous decision in 67% of cases.
You can help prevent indoctrination and help your children resist alienation attempts by paying very close attention to your children's behaviour toward you and by documenting everything you notice meticulously. If your high-conflict ex-spouse attempts to turn your children against you, you must bring it to the Court's attention as soon as possible. You will need the detailed documentation.

It may very well be the case that the judge does not take it seriously or doesn't know how to handle it. You may not have the experts lined up to prove the damage it's doing to your kids, but there's another important reason that you need to bring it out into the open you need to be able to talk to your children about what is happening and you need to be able to counter the lies that are being told about you. Exposure and truth are the only way to begin to reverse this kind of indoctrination, and often it comes down to whether you can prove to your kids that they are being lied to—this is mind control, and your wife has gotten a head start.

More than likely your kids will think you are the one who is lying if you say anything that is contrary to what their mother has said. If you do not bring this to the Court's attention, you're taking a big risk if you talk to your kids about what's happening and start telling them the truth to counter the alienation. This is one more thing that could be used against you in court when your wife complains about you violating the court orders by talking to the kids and disparaging her.

2. Making Your Case. It is true that the legal system for the most part does not have the stomach to remove a child from the alienating parent he or she most closely identifies with, even though it's a very unhealthy alliance. It's also very, very difficult to prove alienation, and there is a lot of controversy about the concept. As a result, there is a tendency for judges to flat-out refuse to consider claims of alienation in fact, the mere mention of the word "alienation" is usually enough to raise a judge's hackles. Claims of parental alienation are often viewed with suspicion and doubt because "parental alienation" has become a trendy catch-phrase that is sometimes used by parents as an excuse to avoid their responsibilities to their kids.

Talk the Talk while you make a good move.

When making your case to a judge, unless it is a judge who is well known to be pro-active in cases of parental alienation, it's usually better to describe the problem in terms such as "the mother is lying to the children and instilling irrational fears about their father" or "the mother is unwilling to co-parent and is excluding the father from their lives" or "the mother is withholding the children during father's time with the children and is damaging their parent-child relationship." All of those descriptions paint a clearer picture than claiming that the mother is alienating the children from their father, which could mean almost anything.

Prove It

You will have to prove your case, and that will require more than just your word against the word of the kids' mother. This is where your documentation will play a vital role. If you have been documenting as they occur the behaviours of your children and your ex-wife, your journals should be admissible as evidence. The fact that you have consistently journaled about these events lends credibility to the testimony you're presenting to the judge. It will often be the case that you don't know exactly what your ex has said or done to cause the change in your children. In these cases, it's important that you document in detail what is going on with your children.

Pay particular attention to comments your children make that sound like they have been rehearsed or which sound awkward and unlike the type of things that children say spontaneously. For instance, if you tell your child that you look forward to seeing them on the weekend and your child says in response, "You're so irresponsible, you probably won't even pick me up" it's probably something your child has heard from their other parent. An 8-year old is not likely to spontaneously conclude that his father is "irresponsible" and would not describe it in those terms. If your child refers to you as "unstable," "abusive," "erratic," "labile," "narcissistic," "lazy," etc., those terms have likely been implanted through repetition by their other parent. Kids don't come up with these concepts on their own. Document the exact words that your child uses as well as the context in which these things are said. While journaling about these behaviours and attitudes of your children, note how the behaviours are different compared to a time before the alienation started and note the lack of any precipitating event that would give rise to these attitudes. Also note how it makes you feel as a parent

Be a Perfect Parent. Well, no one is perfect, right? But, especially while you're fighting this battle, you have to be as close to perfect as possible. That means don't ever miss your visitation and don't ever miss an opportunity to connect with your children. As long as you are not restrained from seeing them or placed on supervised visitation, you do not have to limit your contact to every other weekend or whatever your orders provide.

Establish a regular presence at the kids' schools because their mother will be smearing you to the teachers and school administrators; if those folks can observe for themselves that you're a loving, caring parent and not a hump-backed ogre, they cannot as easily be roped into believing lies about you. If they are called to testify in court, it will be hard for them to say negative things about you if they have their own positive experience of you.

Go have lunch with your kids at school; sneak them encouraging or silly notes in their lockers; send them cards in the mail; set up email accounts for them that their mother cannot access; purchase cell phones for the kids and keep their plans up to date so there is an open line of communication; be available and always put them first; don't be late picking them up; always keep your promises to them; be at every game, concert, recital, open house, etc.; show up at practices or rehearsals and get to know coaches and instructors. The more time you spend with them the better because when they are experiencing you live and in person on a regular basis, it will be harder for negative perceptions of you to take hold.

As tempting as it may be, do not talk negatively about their mother—particularly not in a spiteful or gratuitous way. That's not to say that you cannot correct lies their mother tells them, but you cannot just come out and call their mother a liar—it will be a conversation stopper. This kind of discussion with your children may best be handled with the help of a professional counsellor. Again, be careful about the professionals you choose because if you select someone who is not experienced in dealing with alienation issues, you could actually further the alienation process rather than alleviate it.

I typically recommend that clients participate with their children in family counselling when alienation has started to affect a child's attitude and behaviour toward the target parent. In that case, your child will have some irrational beliefs about you that you will probably find maddening. Communication will be difficult, and your child may refuse to even talk about it with you, in which case you should not force the issue—but you also cannot afford to drop the issue altogether. Get professional assistance to guide the conversations. You may find yourself feeling anger toward your child because behavior such as this hurts and feels like betrayal. It is not your child's fault and you cannot direct your anger at your child—this will further alienate him. Your child is bein

FSC
www.fsc.org
MIX
Papier aus verantwortungsvollen Quellen
Paper from responsible sources
FSC® C105338

Printed by Books on Demand GmbH, Norderstedt / Germany